FOREST OF DISCORD

FOREST OF DISCORD

Options for Governing Our National Forests and Federal Public Lands

Donald W. Floyd, Editor

Kelsey Alexander, Charles Burley, Arthur W. Cooper,
Arthur DuFault, Ross W. Gorte, Sharon G. Haines,
Bruce B. Hronek, Chadwick D. Oliver, Edward W. Shepard

Society of American Foresters

Copyright © 1999 Society of American Foresters

Published by
The Society of American Foresters
5400 Grosvenor Lane
Bethesda, MD 20814-2198
www.safnet.org
(301) 897-8720
(301) 897-3690 fax

ISBN 0-939970-78-3

Printed in the United States of America
10   9   8   7   6   5   4   3   2   1

Library of Congress Cataloging-in-Publication Data

Forest of discord : options for governing our national forests and federal public lands / Donald W. Floyd, editor…[et al.].
         p. cm.
      ISBN 0-93-997078-3
         1. Forest reserves—Management—Government policy—United States.
2. Public lands—Management—Government policy—United States. 3. United States. Forest Service. 4. United States. Bureau of Land Management. I. Floyd, Donald W., 1951–
SD565 .F55 1999
333.75'150973—dc21   99-14849
                                                                      CIP

CONTENTS

TABLES

PREFACE

In October 1976 Congress passed and President Ford signed the two most comprehensive modern laws dealing with the national forests and the public lands administered by the Bureau of Land Management. Although enacting legislation provides a useful benchmark for analysis, it rarely results in resolution of difficult public policy issues.

The many attempts to find consensus on public forest policy notwithstanding, the disparate interests that compete for the products and values produced on our federal forests and rangelands will continue to compete because many of the things they seek are mutually exclusive. Professional resource managers and many members of the public understand the trade-offs that are inherent in the demands that we place on our national forests and public lands. The difficulty comes in the choosing. Which processes shall we use to allocate the resources and values? Which values are most important?

Since its beginnings as an organization intended to advance the science of forestry, the Society of American Foresters (SAF) has struggled with the nonscientific nature of the values that drive the profession. The Society became increasingly involved in public policy issues during the late teens and early 1920s. Barrington Moore chaired the committee that formulated SAF's first statement on forest policy; SAF's council adopted the statement in 1931. Since that time, SAF has attempted to use broadly written statements to guide its process for taking positions.

Over the past 20 years, debate over the national forests and public lands has intensified, both in Congress and among citizens. Several members of Congress introduced legislation to clarify or change policy on various aspects of federal land management, and SAF saw the need for a nonpartisan analysis of these legislative proposals. In December 1996 SAF President Robert W. Bosworth appointed a task force comprising women and men from different regions and professional settings and gave them the following charges:

• To coordinate SAF members' involvement in considering the potential effect of proposed legislation for Forest Service and Bureau of Land Management lands.

• To address specific issues not covered in current law (and associated regulations) that could be addressed by such legislation.

• To develop relevant interim products and a position statement for review and approval by the SAF Council reflecting the Society's interest and involvement in management of the federal public lands, focusing on, but not limited to, the Forest Service and the Bureau of Land Management.

This book, one of several products of the Task Force on Proposed Public Lands Management Legislation, provides background and historical information, a discussion of the issues, criteria for policy and decision analysis, and relevant data about Forest Service and Bureau of Land Management lands. Although our analysis was prompted by the principal current legislation dealing with federal land management issues—S1253, the Public Lands Management Improvement Act of 1997 introduced by Senator Larry Craig (R-Idaho) in the 105th Congress and likely to be reintroduced in the 106th—we have provided the background necessary to analyze other bills dealing with federal land management. We conclude with recommendations for transforming the way our national forests and public lands are managed.

As we point out, the history of public land management in the United States is dominated by disagreement. One of the most important activities that members and leaders of the SAF can undertake is building effective political coalitions for the conservation and management of our public forests and rangelands. Strengthening the capability of foresters to participate in local land management planning processes and to build coalitions within the community may ultimately be the most effective strategy for influencing public forest policy. SAF's council, state societies, and executive vice-president should consider and implement strategies to increase its regional and local chapters' participation in local forest decisionmaking. Coupled with effective national and regional policy representation, such an effort would help the Society speak effectively as the voice of professional forest resource management.

As we debate the issues, it is important to remember that thousands of women and men spend their lives in dedicated service to our national forests and public lands. Their work brings honor to us all and provides an important reminder of what is truly important as we discuss broad questions of policy.

We hope that all readers—natural resource professionals, environmentalists, policymakers, interested citizens—will view this study as a beginning of discussion and dialogue that will lead, ultimately, to effective change.

ACKNOWLEDGMENTS

This work reflects the collective wisdom of many members of the Society of American Foresters. I am particularly indebted to my coauthors, the members of the SAF Task Force on Proposed Public Lands Management Legislation, for their more than two years of dedicated volunteer service. In addition to the task force members themselves, more than 40 reviewers from a variety of agencies, committees, and organizations commented on drafts of the manuscript. Their comments markedly improved our work. Of course, the errors and sins of omission and commission are my responsibility alone.

Although it is always difficult to name some individuals and not others, I want to express my personal gratitude to Susan Cripps for her contribution to the outputs section, and to Robert Malmsheimer for his help on appeals and litigation. Michael Goergen of the SAF national office staff deserves particular praise for providing enthusiasm, optimism, and excellent staff support for our efforts.

My coauthors and I look forward to the debate that this book will engender within the Society of American Foresters, the natural resources management agencies, the legislature, and the administration. We offer this collective work to you, the reader, in the hope that it will stimulate productive change in the ways that we manage this vital American legacy.

—Donald W. Floyd
Editor and Chair
Society of American Foresters Task Force
on Proposed Public Lands Management Legislation

1

A Tradition of Discord

The prevailing values of the American people, expressed through the actions of Congress and the president, have determined the policies by which the federal lands are administered and managed. The values that Americans hold with respect to their forests and the benefits that can be derived from them have changed significantly over our 225-year history.

In the early days of the nation the forest was valued almost entirely for its tangible products—timber, fuel, and game. The forest was also viewed negatively because it sheltered indigenous people who occupied land that had to be cleared for the needs of a mercantile economy (Cronon 1983). These attitudes were reflected in early policies for the federal lands, which encouraged dispossession of Native Americans, agricultural development, and exploitation of timber and mineral resources to support rapid economic expansion. Congress viewed the public lands as an asset that could be sold to raise revenue.

As settlers spread into the continent, Native Americans were dispossessed, natural resources were heavily exploited, and new values emerged. Although some lands were reserved for federal needs from the beginning, the shift from the general disposal policy to retention for preservation and conservation began in 1832, when the reservation of

1

Hot Springs, Arkansas, was established. In 1864 Congress gave Yo-Semite to the state of California with the proviso that it be preserved as a public pleasuring ground (it was returned to federal ownership and management in 1906), and in 1872 Congress created Yellowstone National Park. The roots of the national forests can be found in the Creative Act of 1891, which authorized the president to set aside public lands as forest reserves. In 1897 Congress passed the Organic Administration Act, which specified the purposes for which forest reserves might be established and provided for their protection and management.

That series of congressional actions embodied concerns for the continued availability of forest benefits, for the protection of the forest for its landscape-stabilizing influence, and for the protection of the forest for its beauty and wild properties. This last value, though not so widely held at first, led to preservation of forests wholly for their natural properties, entirely apart from any material benefits they might produce. All these emerging values led to reservation of large areas of federal land, some for commodity production and some for preservation of natural values. Through the vision of Bernhard Fernow, Gifford Pinchot, and other early foresters, the sciences dealing with the ecology and management of natural resources evolved.

In the 20th century, world wars, economic depression, rapid growth, continued distrust of government, demands for new rights, and public participation have influenced American values toward natural resources. Where once public resource management decisions were dominated by a few prevailing values, we now find numerous values, many of which often conflict with one another. Oliver et al. (1997) have divided these diverse current values into two categories:

Desired conditions of the forests. This category includes values associated with sustaining growth of the forest, such as minimizing the effects of exotic and native insects and diseases, minimizing catastrophic levels of native mammals, fire, and natural events; sustaining the global environment; minimizing concentrations of CO_2 and other pollutants; ensuring plant and animal survival and diversity; and ensuring productivity of future forests.

Contributions of the forest to the quality of human life. These include timber products, nontimber and nonwildlife products, reserved (preserved) areas, recreational opportunities, commodity- and noncommodity-dependent rural lifestyles, the capability of the forest to support economic activity, water volume and usefulness, game and nongame fish and wildlife, the economic viability of the private landowner forest sector, concerns with the costs of managing forest lands, spiritual and cultural values, and scenic, existence and historical values.

In one form or another, virtually all of those values are reflected in our current disagreements over management of the federal lands.

Reasons for Policy Change

Since the United States began acquiring new lands over 200 years ago, certain policy issues have been relevant to the disposition, use, and management of these lands. Clawson (1983) identifies eight questions, paraphrased as follows:

1. How much land should the national government acquire?

2. Of the land acquired by the federal government, how much should be disposed of and how much should be retained?

3. Assuming that at least some land will be disposed of, to whom should the disposals be made?

4. If permanent or temporary disposal is chosen, on what terms shall the federal lands be made available?

5. If the decision is made to retain permanent title in the federal government for at least some land but also to permit private use, what conditions shall be imposed on such use?

6. How much effort and how many federal dollars shall be expended to conserve or preserve the federal lands?

7. What sort of relationship should exist among the federal, state, and local governments in the management of the federal lands and in the sharing of revenues from them?

8. How shall the planning for the use, management, disposal, retention, and other aspects of federal lands be carried out?

The first four questions have been the subject of policy debates in the recent past, but at present, they do not seem to be generating enough political support to advance beyond occasional proposals by interest groups, local governments, academics, and sporadic bills in Congress. The last four questions, however, form the basis for a lively debate that has drawn the attention of Congress, the administration, the states, and interest groups.

Over time, answers to those policy questions have changed with changes in public values and political culture. What may once have been appropriate may not be appropriate now. The challenges for professional natural resource managers are analyzing the past and current situations, determining, in light of prevailing values, what changes in policy are appropriate for the foreseeable future, and recommending legislative and executive actions to accomplish these changes.

The National Forests

The forest reserves (now the national forests) were authorized in the Creative Act of 1891 in response to citizens' outcry concerning what they perceived as wanton destruction of forests on the public domain and subsequent downstream flooding. Congress gave President Benjamin Harrison the authority to withdraw federal lands from entry under the various homestead acts, and in 1891 he created the Yellowstone Reserve (now the Shoshone National Forest). He and his successors used the withdrawal authority from time to time, but the power was not used extensively until President Theodore Roosevelt tripled the amount of land reserved, from 46.5 million acres to 172.2 million acres.

The Organic Administration Act of 1897 established the purposes of the forest reserves:"to improve and protect the forest within the boundaries, or for the purpose of securing favorable conditions of water flows, and to furnish a continuous supply of timber for the use and necessities of the citizens of the United States." The act was part of an appropriations bill and was largely intended to restrict the authority of the president to reserve lands. Records of congressional floor debate from 1891 to 1897 indicate the lands were intended to be set aside principally to prevent their exploitation. This same debate also shows that the timber was expected to be used primarily by homesteaders and miners for personal use, rather than for the development of a timber industry. Lands more valuable for minerals or agricultural purposes were not to be included among reserved lands. The law also empowered the secretary of Interior, who then had jurisdiction, to establish regulations for the use of the several resources of the national forests (Steen 1997).

Congress made an important policy decision concerning the relationship between the national forests and local governments when it enacted the Twenty-Five Percent Fund Act of 1908. This law allocates 25 percent of revenues to the states for use on roads and schools in the counties where national forests are located. The states were allowed to determine which road and school programs were funded, but the level and allocation were determined by the Forest Service. Floor debate on both the 1908 act and its 1907 predecessor, which set revenue sharing at 10 percent, made it clear that Congress enacted the provision as a substitute for property taxes because the national forests were exempt from local taxation. No mention was made of why 25 percent (or 10 percent in 1907) was the appropriate share. In 1976 the National Forest Management Act (NFMA) redefined gross revenues (the base for revenue sharing) to include deposits to the Knutson-Vandenberg fund and purchaser road credits, thus increasing payments to counties.

Although numerous laws concerning the national forests were passed after 1908, there were no further statements of management policy until 1960, when Congress passed the Multiple Use Sustained Yield Act (MUSY). This act states,

> It is the policy of the Congress that the national forests are established and shall be administered for outdoor recreation, range, timber, watershed, and wildlife and fish purposes.... The establishment and maintenance of areas of wilderness are consistent with the purposes and provisions of this Act.

The purposes of MUSY were declared "supplemental to, and not in derogation of, the purposes for which the national forests were established as set forth in [the 1897 Organic Act]." In addition to broadening the base of resources for which the National Forest System could be managed, essentially giving statutory blessing to what the Forest Service was already doing, MUSY added management direction. It then defined multiple use:

> ... management of all the various renewable surface resources of the national forests so that they are utilized in the combination that will best meet the needs of the American people ... harmonious and coordinated management of the various resources ... [giving consideration] to the relative values of the various resources, and not necessarily the combination of uses that will give the greatest dollar return or the greatest unit output.

The act also called for sustained-yield management, defined as "the achievement and maintenance in perpetuity of a high-level annual or regular periodic output of the various renewable resources without impairment of the productivity of the land."

The 1974 Forest and Rangeland Renewable Resources Planning Act (RPA) and NFMA in 1976 added significant planning and public participation requirements to national forest management. Although a section of the Organic Act dealing with timber harvest practices was repealed, neither act changed management philosophy in a significant way. Nonetheless, the fact that NFMA was largely a timber regulation law, inspired by timber issues, probably contributed significantly to the Forest Service's management emphasis on timber outputs.

Thus, the National Forest System is managed under three separate policies, the first of which is more than 100 years old. These laws and their interpretation have established the system as a timber reserve where management for water flows, grazing, recreation, wildlife and fish, and wilderness is authorized. Management for the outputs is to be coordinated so that they are produced in the combination and amounts that "best meet the needs of the American people," without necessarily maximizing economic return, and in a manner that can be sustained in perpetuity. Under the General Mining Law and the Mineral Leasing Act, the allocations are complicated by mineral production, which in many cases dominates other uses. Such a system of management requires intensive planning and extensive public review.

The Bureau of Land Management

The Bureau of Land Management (BLM) is responsible for the public domain, the grazing districts, and the Oregon and California Railroad lands. The public domain and grazing districts are largely grassland and desert that were neither divested nor reserved for any other federal purpose and were overseen by the General Land Office. The General Land Office was established in 1812 to supervise disposal of the public domain. It also oversaw the forest reserves from the time they were created until the Transfer Act of 1905 moved them to the US Department of Agriculture.

Management of these lands was not authorized until 1934, when the Taylor Grazing Act passed and the Grazing Service was created to implement the requirements of the law. The Taylor Act essentially shifted the emphasis from disposal to retention while ostensibly deferring a decision on eventual disposal of the remaining public domain. During its short existence, the Grazing Service encountered many difficulties, some of which can reasonably be interpreted as political interference from western congressional interests and internecine squabbling between the Departments of Agriculture and Interior. Consequently, in 1946 the Grazing Service and the General Land Office were combined to form BLM. From its inception, and because of the nature of its lands, BLM emphasized mineral production—by law, the "highest and best use" of these lands—and grazing, and to a lesser extent, timber management. BLM was charged by statute with supervising mineral production on its own lands and those of other federal agencies. Because of its organization into statewide regions, BLM has been subject to pressures from state governments and congressional delegations that the National Forest System has sometimes avoided.

From its creation, BLM lacked policy direction in the form of an organic act. Congress first attempted to give the agency direction in the Multiple Use and Land Classification Act of 1964. The law directed multiple-use, sustained-yield management of the public lands pending implementation of the recommendations of the Public Land Law Review Commission. The commission presented its report, entitled *One Third of the*

Nation's Land, in 1970. Congress debated the results of the report for six years before passing the Federal Land Policy and Management Act of 1976 (FLPMA). The act states that the BLM-administered public lands should be retained in federal ownership and managed "on the basis of multiple use and sustained yield unless otherwise specified by law," that management should protect environmental and aesthetic values, that where appropriate, management "will preserve and protect certain public lands in their natural condition" (i.e., as wilderness), and that the United States should receive fair market value of the use of the public lands and their resources unless otherwise provided for by statute. The act also required a land-use planning process but provided little policy direction for the decisions to be made during such planning. The law also repealed or modified most of the laws permitting disposal of land under old statutes.

Revenue sharing on the public domain lands is substantially more complex than on national forests. There are a multitude of payment programs, depending on the history and location of the land and the nature and type of the land or resource sale. They include mineral leases and permits, lands and materials (including timber), grazing, and other miscellaneous sources. In addition, there are payments in lieu of taxes to counties calculated under a complex formula prescribed in law, most recently in the Payments in Lieu of Taxes Act of 1976, as amended in 1994.

The most important forest resources managed by the BLM are the Oregon and California Railroad lands. In 1916 Congress revoked the title to more than 2 million acres that it had granted to the Oregon and California Railroad (gradually absorbed by the Southern Pacific Railroad) in 1869. In 1919 Congress also reclaimed title to more than 93,000 acres originally granted to the state of Oregon for the construction of the Coos Bay Military Wagon Road in southwestern Oregon. These lands, collectively known as the O&C lands, contained some of the most productive forests in the Pacific Northwest. The revestiture was prompted by gross violations of the original conditions of the land grant, falsification of records, bribery, and other malfeasance by the holders of the grant (Richardson 1980). Following revestiture, the General Land Office began classifying the lands and offering them for sale at auction. Sales were not strong. The agency was criticized for its administration of the project, and the Forest Service, which managed national forests intermingled with the O&C lands, sought but did not win overall jurisdiction. In the Oregon and California Revested Lands Sustained Yield Management Act of 1937, Congress required the General Land Office to manage for sustained yield:

> These lands shall be managed...for permanent forest production, and the timber thereon shall be sold, cut and removed in conformity with the princi-

pal of sustained yield for...providing a permanent source of timber supply, protecting watersheds, regulating stream flow, and contributing to the economic stability of local communities and industries (Dana 1956).

The act is important because it was the first time that the federal government had formally adopted the notion of sustainability. As successor to the General Land Office, the Bureau of Land Management acquired jurisdiction over these lands in the late 1940s. Congress gave the counties in which the O&C lands occur 75 percent of the gross receipts minus the costs of road construction and reforestation, up to 25 percent. In reality, road and reforestation costs have always taken 25 percent, so the counties effectively got 50 percent of the gross revenues. In 1993 Congress changed the formula for funding,[1] but these lands continue to be a major source of revenue for local governments in western Oregon.

Public Values and Policy Change

The major statutes governing the national forests and public lands reflect the public values and perceptions of their time. In the late 1800s the nation had experienced almost 100 years of unabated forest clearing attended by extensive fires and floods. Although influential citizens finally convinced Congress that such abuses portended a serious shortage of timber, it was water flow and flooding that influenced Congress most in its debates over creation of the forest reserves. The Organic Act thus reflected deep public concern with resource destruction and depletion. Similarly, Congress was inspired to protect and manage the public domain lands by the 1930s dust bowl—perhaps quite literally. The story goes that during the floor debate on the Taylor Grazing Act, a windstorm deposited dust from the Great Plains on the Capitol, and when the dust settled, the act was passed.

The Multiple Use Sustained Yield Act of 1960 reflected its own times, a period of rapid economic growth and heavy demand on resources fueled by the end of World War II. It was largely a Forest Service proposal prompted by unprecedented pressures from interest groups, including ranchers, the timber industry, the housing industry, and wilderness advo-

---

[1]In 1993 (§13893 of the Omnibus Budget Reconciliation Act of 1993 as amended by P.L. 103-443), Congress established a 10-year program (fiscal years 1994–2003) of payments based on a share of average payments for fiscal years 1986–1990, beginning at 85 percent in 1994 and declining by 3 percentage points annually to 58 percent in 2003 for the O&C lands. (A parallel program was also established for the counties where national forest timber programs were affected by northern spotted owl protection.) The counties, however, can choose payments under this formula or their regular (50 percent) payments during the last five years of the program (fiscal years 1999–2003).

cates, and by competition with the National Park Service over recreation. Although timber production had been growing in importance all along, it was during the postwar period that the national forests changed from timber reserves to major sources of timber for companies whose own holdings had been diminished by the demands of war and the subsequent economic boom (Robbins 1997).

The Forest Service has long had an economic development vision. Long-term timber contracts in southeastern Alaska were first offered in the 1920s, in an effort to stimulate development of a timber industry (Steen 1976). It took until the 1950s for the Forest Service to find companies interested in fulfilling the associated 50-year contract requirements of building pulp mills. In some areas, particularly the northern Rocky Mountains and the Pacific Northwest, entire communities grew dependent on timber and other resources from national forests and public lands. The economic stability of these "dependent communities" has become a major issue in public resource policy.

Timber cutting on the national forests clearly had both positive and negative effects. Users of other resources demanded that their interests be given priority when management decisions for the national forests were made. However, resource limitations were ill perceived, and the major policy problem lay in managing uses and outputs so that the demands of each interest could be satisfied. The answer seemed to lie in a more coordinated system of resource management, in which multiple uses would be considered collectively and outputs optimized. Demands could be met and conflicts resolved by spatially or temporally separating incompatible uses. Concern for the future was reflected in the sustained-yield provisions of MUSY. In practice this concern appears to have been interpreted more as a policy guide than as a constraint that should dominate management. MUSY reflected the growth-dominated attitudes of Congress and the public just as clearly as did the huge public works programs of the 1960s. Furthermore, fiscal constraints were not yet issues.

By the mid-1970s, when NFMA and FLPMA were passed, the environmental movement had gained considerable political influence. The impacts of the intensive resource management practiced during the 1950s and early 1960s had become evident, and significant sectors of the public were demanding changes in forest policy. Much of the debate over these two laws (particularly NFMA) centered on what such practices as clearcutting were doing to the national forests and the fate of the public lands in the absence of policy direction from Congress. Other environmental issues involved livestock grazing and the amounts of timber, particularly old-growth, that should be cut from Forest Service lands.

An equally important theme in the discussions of the 1970s was citizen empowerment and public participation in the planning process. This debate was only a microcosm of a wider movement following the Vietnam War, the Civil Rights Movement, and Watergate to increase citizens' control over government run amok. Citizens' involvement in federal land management was also a result of the National Environmental Policy Act of 1969 (NEPA). The planning processes called for in NFMA and FLPMA reflect the desire of citizens to influence agency decisions and the desire of Congress to direct, albeit in a limited way, how those resources should be managed.

The Environment of Policymaking Today

As in the past, today's debate about public management policies reflects current knowledge and values. We now know more about the complexities of resource management than we did when our national forest and public land systems were established. The decisions of the Forest Service and the Department of the Interior to stress ecosystem management as their management paradigm reflect advances in our understanding of the complexity of forest and rangeland systems and the interrelated nature of management decisions and system outcomes.

The debate over ecosystem management also suggests that past decisions under the multiple-use paradigm led to levels of commodity production and environmental degradation that now seem less acceptable in light of current public values. The neologism itself, ecosystem management, is perhaps necessary to signal the shift toward greater environmental consideration in decisionmaking about national forests and public lands.

In the last 25 years, the environmental movement has taken deeper root, expanding both its knowledge about environmental issues and its political power and the willingness to exercise it. The power of environmental and other interest groups, so prevalent in other areas of political life, is equally strong in public lands policy. No single set of values predominates in the public debate. Environmental and commodity interests are engaged in a struggle over how to manage the national forests and public lands, with each side seeking advantage through elected officials and administrators who are sensitive to their concerns. Some citizens believe that no timber should be harvested from these lands, and others believe that harvesting more timber is appropriate. We have entered a time when the public demands to be included in government decisionmaking, and land managers who ignore the interested public take a considerable risk.

The policymaking environment itself seems to have changed nearly as much as public values and our knowledge of ecology. Citizen empowerment, interest group influence, and administrative authority have increased markedly. More interests are involved and they speak with greater volume and sophistication. Decisions of the Forest Service and BLM are challenged through the administrative appeals process or the courts, and natural resource policies are the subjects of strenuous debate in Congress. The issues are more complex, the values more diverse, the financial stakes greater.

Scientific and technological innovation has created a knowledge base vastly different from the one that existed when most laws governing the federal lands were enacted. The concept of ecosystems and our knowledge of these systems, although yet imperfect, suggest a management paradigm fundamentally different from (but not incompatible with) the multiple uses and sustained yields envisioned in the 1950s and early 1960s. Management science is more sophisticated than it was just 20 years ago, and the technology available to today's resource manager, although sometimes a mixed blessing, has the potential to revolutionize both planning and on-the-ground management.

Perhaps the one thing that has not changed is the polarization of regions and interests: federal resource professionals continue to manage land absent a consensus of values among the landowners.

The conflict of interests and values and rapidly changing conditions suggest that it is time to reconsider our policies for managing the national forests and public lands—policies that are 25 to 100 years old and were implemented under different scientific, social, and political circumstances. Change seems imminent. The challenge is ensuring a place for reasoned discussion and professional discretion in the proposed solutions.

Policy Issues

A number of significant issues must be considered in legislative and regulatory reform of public land management. Some of these issues are matters of fact, but more are rooted in differing values. This section outlines the critical policy issues that successful legislative and regulatory reform must address. We first treat several conceptual problems in federal land management and then discuss a variety of administrative and organizational issues.

Overarching Issues

At least three issues that affect the Forest Service and Bureau of Land Management (BLM) result from the structure of our government and the nature of our institutions: the desire of interest groups to reduce uncertainty, the inherent limitations of planning, and the effects of divided government. These issues, which profoundly shape the debate over federal land policy and management, are unlikely to change without fundamental structural changes in our government and economic institutions.

The desire of interest groups to reduce uncertainty. Interest groups increasingly seek to reduce uncertainty in the production of outputs and the future conditions of the land; they also seek to prevail. For example, the forest products industry must make investment and management decisions based on predictions of the availability of raw materials. Where federal lands predominate in the ownership mix, public forest policy and management decisions strongly affect industry viability. Similarly, commercial outdoor recreation interests face uncertainty with access and wilderness regulations. Interest groups concerned about water supply, wilderness, wildlife habitat management, livestock grazing, and ecosystem protection all seek to reduce the uncertainty associated with promoting their interests on the national forests and public lands.

Although humans often seek certainty through resource planning and management (Behan 1975), ecosystems are dynamic, constantly changing in response to a variety of human and nonhuman disturbances. Managing to sustain vigorous, productive ecosystems and predictable flows of commodities and amenities is exceedingly complex. Legislation, which sets the policies for natural resources management, must acknowledge this complexity and recognize that in many situations there are trade-offs among producing continuous high levels of commodities, maximizing ecosystem resilience, and protecting amenities.

The limitations of planning. There is an assumption embedded in the Resources Planning Act (RPA) and the National Forest Management Act (NFMA), and to a lesser extent the Federal Land Policy and Management Act (FLPMA), that resource planning and citizen participation can resolve resource management conflicts. All three laws rely on complex planning processes to resolve conflicting demands. "Planning is an inherently political exercise. And because of this political nature there will always be unfulfilled expectations, multiple and conflicting goals, institutional constraints and limits to goal accomplishment" (Cortner and Shannon 1993).

Rather than resolve underlying differences, the planning process has provided an additional arena for interest-based struggle. Once resources are allocated through decisions based on an approved plan, individual management decisions become the focus of the disagreements. Congress, in attempting to avoid difficult policy choices, ratified the use of a planning process designed by the Forest Service. The agency believed that if given enough discretion, it could make decisions rationally. In reality, by ratifying the Forest Service's proposal, Congress sanctioned a complex planning process, shifting conflict to a different level.

Although the Forest Service had argued that if given sufficient latitude, it could resolve conflicts rationally, several analysts were skeptical. Behan (1981) wrote,

> What do we have in general and abstract terms? A planning process as close to the classic rational and comprehensive model, and as close to per-

fection as human imagination can design and implement. The legislation is long and detailed; the regulations added much specificity; the adopted procedures and FORPLAN [a computer program]... are rational and comprehensive and at least theoretically rigorous and invincible; and the training manual for planning teams highlights and prescribes the very latest in mathematical, conceptual and analytical elegance.

Gregg (1992) compared complex national planning efforts to the failure of the Soviet Union:

> Planning has become a major part of the problem. We've set up planning systems which are based on the assumption—surely childlike faith in the face of collapse of elaborate planning in most of the other societies of the world— that somehow or other if we just get planning that is comprehensive enough, looks far enough into the future, is formal enough and costs enough money, it will produce agreement on action. There is absolutely nothing in history to suggest that is true.

Federal land managers, commodity interests, and environmental advocates seem stalemated. Some industry advocates believe that they have compromised their demands only to be asked to give up more as a result of administrative and court challenges from environmental groups. The environmentalists, in turn, contend that the land management agencies have been "captured" by the timber and livestock industries. As a result, public land managers suffer from what can best be described as "the beaten dog syndrome" (Germain and Floyd 1996): they receive the equivalent of a beating for nearly every proposed action from at least one interest group.

A few observers in the media have noticed this difficulty. Although some readers may question the details in the following newspaper article (Fisher 1997, p. 10A), it accurately reflects the larger problem of federal managers who are caught in the middle.

> Organizations like the Natural Resources Defense Council will not be happy until every tree on every national forest is declared off limits to the timber industry. The industry, once habituated to buying 200 year-old Tongass spruces for $2.00 each, will not be satisfied until the Tongass returns to the logging limit of old, about twice that of the new plan. And both sides blame the Forest Service. The blame is misplaced. When the Forest Service turns to compromises like the Tongass plan, it only acknowledges and tries to accommodate opposing clans of a public-opinion feud over the future of our great forests. And if anything the feud is growing more unyielding. Consider the recent vote by members of the Sierra Club to oppose all logging on national forests...
>
> Americans expect the agencies of their government to reflect their own wishes, but when those agencies are presented with such widely disparate wishes, both held by such wide segments of the populace, they have no choice but to seek a middle course. In this instance, the Forest Service de-

serves better. Not only for trying to chart that course, but for doing so amid a
continuous crossfire. If anyone is to be scolded, it is the Hatfields and, of
course the McCoys.

Rational comprehensive planning has not (and probably cannot) resolve the underlying disputes that drive public forest management conflicts. It is important for those involved to understand that conflict over
management of natural resources is fundamental, inevitable, and within
some limits, healthy (Floyd 1993).

Proposals to shape federal lands policy have been highly controversial
since the time of the Articles of Confederation. It seems unlikely that
peace will break out in the near future as a result of better planning regulations. Federal forest and rangeland management is likely to continue to
be contentious. Two important questions are whether the conflicts can
be managed productively and at what scale we will attempt to manage
them.

The effect of divided government. There is an intentional tension in our
government between Congress and the executive. Congress often has a
tendency to regard executive direction to executive agencies as political
meddling. At the same time, Congress attempts to control the agencies
through prescriptive legislation and set policy through the appropriations process, as when House and Senate leaders recently asked the chief
of the Forest Service to provide information so that their committees
could consider directing the agency to undertake "custodial management" of the National Forest System (Murkowski et al. 1998).

Forest industry and environmental groups continue to enjoy direct access to the executive agencies and congressional committees. Their competing agendas are often reflected in the policy proposals that emerge
from the executive and Congress. As the Salvage Rider of 1995 and the
proposed roads moratorium illustrate, federal lands policy is often whip-
sawed by the competing agendas of the political parties, the legislature,
and the executive. Over time, these changes in course mark the bounds
of public lands policy. In the short term, they create the appearance of
chaotic governance.

Legislative Issues

The following section sets out a series of fundamental policy issues
that are within the purview of Congress. The property clause of the US
Constitution makes Congress responsible for writing the laws necessary
to guide management of the national forests and public lands. Policies
such as multiple use, sustained yield, protection of endangered species,

and conservation of water resources are the result of statutes that Congress has passed. The legislature has also been primarily responsible for promoting public participation and providing the financial framework for managing federal lands.

Mission. In its report on Forest Service decisionmaking (GAO 1997a, p. 5), the General Accounting Office noted,

> Strengthening accountability for performance within the Forest Service and improving the efficiency and effectiveness of its decision-making is contingent on establishing long-term strategic goals that are based on clearly defined mission priorities. However, agreement does not exist on the agency's long-term strategic goals. This lack of agreement is the result of a more fundamental disagreement, both inside and outside the Forest Service, over which uses the agency is to emphasize under its broad multiple-use and sustained-yield mandate and how best to ensure the long-term sustainability of these issues.

Few would argue that the agency's mission is clearly defined. In its 1997 draft strategic plan, the Forest Service stated that its current mission is to "achieve quality land management under sustainable multiple use management concepts to meet the diverse needs of the land and people" (GAO 1997b, p. 9) Organizations that perform well have a clear sense of direction, and their managers have a strong vision of where they need to go and why. This requires a strategic mission. A clearly defined mission provides the basis for establishing an organization's direction and what it needs to do to get there.

Defining the mission is just one part of management. The agency must also establish targets and objectives, formulate a strategy to achieve them, execute the plan, and compare its performance against its mission and targets.

To some extent the Bureau of Land Management has escaped the recent criticisms aimed at the Forest Service. One may speculate that its smaller budget, regional presence, and smaller forest management program provide some protective cover, yet BLM's 1995 mission statement is no clearer than that of the Forest Service: "The Bureau of Land Management sustains the health, diversity, and productivity of the public lands for the use and enjoyment of present and future generations." The definition of multiple use in FLPMA is even more expansive than the one in the Multiple Use Sustained Yield Act (MUSY). Commodity groups, environmentalists, and state and local governments have many of the same interests in the public lands as they do in the national forests, and grazing management has been a particular focus of the environmental groups. But the recent rapid population growth and urbanization of the West virtually guarantee that more and more-active interest groups will compete for the multiple uses of the public lands in the near future.

Agency organization. Since the early 1900s, when the Forest Service was established, the number of federal land management agencies, each with different but in some cases overlapping missions, has grown. The most recent major restructuring of a federal natural resource agency came with changes in what is now the US Fish and Wildlife Service in 1956 and 1970. The clearest duplication of mission is between the Forest Service and BLM. Both administer vast land holdings, both are charged with managing lands according to principles of multiple use, both administer wilderness lands, both administer surface resources (timber and range) that are used by economic interests, and both provide important opportunities for recreation. They are further intertwined by their often adjacent and occasionally intermingled lands and BLM's responsibility for mineral management on Forest Service and other federal lands.

However, the agencies differ in important ways. Whereas the Forest Service administration is centralized in Washington, DC, and in multistate regional offices, BLM is organized with regional offices on a state (occasionally multistate) level. The nature and distribution of the natural resources and their uses also differ.

Suggestions that the Forest Service and BLM be merged have been made in the past (Gorte and Cody 1995), and perhaps it is again appropriate to reexamine how well national interests are served by having two major federal multiple-use land-management agencies as independent entities. A merger would present major policy implications, including fiscal impacts; institutional effects related to agency mores, employment levels, esprit de corps, and different policies in critical areas; legal and political considerations involving policies and jurisdictions; and impacts on service to the public.

There are alternatives short of full merger of the two agencies. One proposal would swap federal resource lands and give forest management to the Forest Service and management of grazing and arid lands to BLM. Defining and implementing administrative responsibility based on predominant cover types, however, would only create a different set of boundary problems. More sweeping proposals would create a single natural resource department with multiple specialized agencies. At this stage, our purpose is not to advance one proposal over another but to point out that any consideration of the policies under which federal lands are managed must include agency structure. There may be many reasons to maintain the current administrative structure, but the current template clearly requires examination.

Land allocation. Natural resources are, by definition, relatively scarce (Randall 1987). In the United States, we allocate natural resources through a combination of market forces and government regulation. On public lands, competition for allocation is an intense and necessarily political process. With the exception of the initial reservation of the national forests and public lands and wartime planning, the United States has largely avoided centralized planning and allocation of natural resources.

Given that the area under public ownership is unlikely to increase or decrease substantially and that human populations and their associated demands will both increase and vary with time, one must eventually confront the public land allocation issue. How much public land should be dedicated to wilderness and how much should be managed for timber? How many acres for watershed protection, for parks and for wildlife habitat? The questions do not have easy answers. Congress has occasionally created new public land classifications (such as wilderness) and reallocated multiple-use lands to such dominant uses as parks, wildlife habitat, and recreation. And the Oregon and California Grant Lands (O&C lands) and the Coos Bay Wagon Road lands are congressionally designated for timber harvest for the stability of nearby communities and forest industry.

The president also has the ability to make land-use decisions through the periodic use of presidential proclamations under the Antiquities Act. President Clinton used this authority to allocate 1.7 million acres as a BLM-managed national monument in Utah, the Grand Staircase Escalante National Monument.

Most of the public lands and national forests, however, remain classified for multiple use, with management allocations made at smaller spatial scales by professional resource managers. Comprehensive public lands management legislation must address the allocation issues. Allocation into dominant uses is often controversial—the legislative backlash that followed establishment of the Grand Staircase Escalante National Monument is a case in point—and viewed by legislators as a lose-lose proposition.

Ecosystem management. In 1993 the Society of American Foresters provided this description of ecosystem management (SAF 1993):

> Ecosystem management approaches sustainability by treating the forest as a hierarchical and complex system of organisms and abiotic components with functional linkages between them. The conditions (or properties) of the forest are the result of the many individual processes within the system and the linkages among them. They exist at different scales and as dynamic entities shaped by natural disturbances such as fires, floods, and storms. Ecosystems do not exhibit clear boundaries, although humans commonly delineate

boundaries to fit political, administrative, research and management needs. These concepts are not entirely new; many aspects have been incorporated in forest ecology classes for more than 40 years. Today, however, they are better understood and accepted as important concepts that should be incorporated in management strategies.

Ecosystem management attempts to maintain the complex processes, pathways and interdependencies intact, and functioning well, over long periods of time. The essence of maintaining ecosystem integrity is to retain the health and resilience of systems so they can accommodate short-term stresses and adapt to long-term change. The key elements include: maintenance of biological diversity and soil fertility; conservation of genetic variation and its dispersal; and through evolution, future biological diversity... Maintenance of these ecological processes and properties sets the bounds within which specific ecosystem management objectives (including sustained-yield of products) can be pursued.

Ecosystem management is not incompatible with multiple use and sustained yield in concept. However, just as we have seen with other complex concepts, questions immediately arise about the implications of the concept for on-the-ground management. These questions are often about establishing priorities. If sustaining forest diversity, fertility, and resilience are the factors that bound production of goods and services, what levels of production are compatible with their sustenance? Comprehensive legislation that seeks to guide the public lands and national forests must acknowledge ecosystem complexity and its relationship to sustained production of goods and services. At what temporal and spatial scale is sustainability to be determined?

Legislative processes to address the application of complex management paradigms have often created new sets of problems; rarely have they resolved the issues they set out to address. It is easier to recognize complexity in authorizing legislation than to set up an appropriations process that makes ecosystem management happen.

Multiple use and sustained yield. Multiple use and sustained yield have been the statutory mandate for managing Forest Service and BLM lands since 1960 and 1976, respectively. These principles express a concept that has been widely accepted by both the agencies and the public. To question it is almost heresy, but many professional resource managers are beginning to acknowledge its limitations. The concept is politically palatable because it expresses a rational basis for allocating public resources and seems to promise everything to everyone. However, some critics argue that the current problems in Forest Service and BLM land management can be laid to difficulties inherent in the multiple-use and sustained-yield principles, particularly the considerable discretion granted to decisionmakers.

One of the most serious problems lies in the scale at which the principles are applied. The language of MUSY refers to the national forests, implying that its principles apply systemwide and that the multiple benefits derive from the system as a whole, not necessarily from each unit of the system. Individuals and interest groups argue that their benefits must be derived from an individual forest, watershed, or ranger district, or even a stand. Although this may be possible at the forest level, it is not at the stand level, where individual, usually dominant-use decisions are made. In fact, at the stand level, some uses, such as timber harvesting and wilderness, are mutually exclusive within limited temporal scales.

Multiple benefits are produced at a large scale as a result of hundreds or thousands of aggregated dominant-use decisions made on a stand scale. That a dominant-use decision to manage for elk habitat may benefit water yield does not change the fact that the decision to manage was driven by the desire to produce elk. Similarly, the multiple benefits that derive from wilderness are by-products of a decision to manage for wilderness. The principle of multiple use works only at relatively large spatial scales. Although the statement may seem self-evident, lack of understanding on this point is at the root of much current dissatisfaction with Forest Service and BLM management.

A problem in the multiple-use concept lies in its apparent promise that the level of benefits desired by one interest can be achieved without reducing the benefits desired by others. Although this may be technically possible when relative abundance of resources occurs, as was the case 40 years ago, such conditions no longer exist. MUSY and FLPMA address scarcity by directing that the resources of the national forests and public lands be used in a combination that will best meet the needs of the American people, not the needs of a particular interest group. Multiple-use decisions by their very nature thus represent compromises, and because they do, proponents of single uses are often disappointed. Few are satisfied and essential political support for the decision often disappears.

Congress itself has undermined implementation of the multiple-use concept by its failure to match budgetary actions with legislative instruction. Repeatedly, the Forest Service has gone to Congress with budget proposals requesting levels of spending for the various resources necessary to achieve "harmonious and coordinated management of the various resources" only to have Congress differentially fund one over another (Mohai et al. 1995). This was particularly frustrating when the Forest Service requests were contained in the RPA program, a document drafted at congressional request. Timber's historically greater share of funding fueled the belief by some that multiple use was more talk than action and that the national forests were, despite MUSY, a timber reserve.

The Forest Service also bears some of the blame for the difficulty of implementing MUSY. Typically, there has been a mismatch between the integrated, multiple-use land and resource management plans and the annual budget requests. In addition, Congress does not make funding decisions in a vacuum. It may not be politically feasible for the agency to tell Congress that given levels of expenditure on timber sales may have impacts on recreation use or fish and wildlife habitat. The Forest Service response to congressional questions about the feasibility of increasing timber sales was often positive (Hirt 1994).

Some critics perceive a gap between what the agencies say they will do when they complete management plans and how the budget is allocated each year. Funds are distributed to programs for timber, wildlife, rangeland, recreation, and so forth, rather than toward managing the ecosystem. The budgeting system is particularly inefficient for ecosystem restoration projects that focus on systemic functions, such as soil, water, and wildlife. A related issue is that integrating planning costs have escalated well above original estimates. Even though the Forest Service has generally received the funds requested for land management planning, it has not delivered the outputs that the plans specify. Some plans have been developed without budget constraints (GAO 1996). This gap between plans and reality means that many of the actions called for in plans and justified on multiple-use grounds can never be realized simply because of a lack of funds.

Two points made in the 1997 General Accounting Office report are significant. First, Congress has consistently modified existing forest plans with directives contained in appropriations bills. Second, because there are numerous trust funds and special accounts, largely funded by timber sale receipts and spent on timber management, many critics believe that timber management has not faced the same fiscal constraints as other program areas. A separate section in this chapter details these trust funds and special accounts.

If those problems were not enough, planning for true multiple-use management is intellectually difficult. Until the advent of computers, it was probably impossible. MUSY calls for a complex balancing of outputs in which no one use dominates, the productivity of the land is not impaired, revenue is not necessarily maximized, and the decision reasonably accords with the public opinion expressed during the analysis. The analysis must combine priced and unpriced goods and services. Furthermore, for the national forests the combination of resources produced must "best meet the needs of the American people." Who can make such a decision and on what basis can it be made? The Forest Service and BLM are filling a vacuum and making political decisions in the guise of technical allocation of resources.

MUSY, NFMA, and FLPMA express lofty goals for the national forests and public lands, but their provisions are vague and easily misunderstood and have been widely interpreted by the agencies. The laws are difficult to implement at a scale below the national forest or BLM district level. If multiple use is to remain the prevailing concept for management of public lands, its principles need to be articulated so that they can be understood and implemented. Congress must understand the effects of funding decisions on the full array of resource values.

No less than multiple use, other broad principles that underlie modern forest management are easily misunderstood. The meanings of ecosystem management, forest health, and sustained yield are unique to each beholder. Because these principles provide no management or action standards, interests will always disagree about what they mean and whether they are being properly implemented. Thus, our debates about these concepts often emphasize our collective lack of agreement rather than an emerging professional consensus.

Overlapping and interacting federal laws. Resource management planning is complicated both because of the dynamic, complex nature of forest and rangeland ecosystems and because of the equally complex legislative and regulatory framework that we impose on resource managers. Forest Service and BLM managers must comply with literally hundreds of statutes, executive orders, and regulations that guide the planning and decisionmaking process. The web of forest policies requires the agencies to establish and maintain elaborate cooperative processes with a host of other federal and state agencies. Because these agencies have different missions, they interpret statutes and regulations differently. The result, too often, is that they fail to agree on land management decisions. In recent cases, land management has been guided as much by decisions of the regulatory agencies as by the resource agencies.

Given the number of federal environmental laws that have been enacted in the past 20 years—bills drafted by different committees of Congress with different motivations—it is hardly surprising that these laws do not mesh well (Appendix 2 lists the major statutes that affect Forest Service and BLM planning and management). The overlapping nature of NFMA, FLPMA, the Endangered Species Act, and the Clean Water and Clean Air Acts, combined with the overarching authority of the National Environmental Policy Act, has made management of the federal lands increasingly complex. The differing cultures of the agencies administering these acts and their particular constituencies further complicate the administrative and managerial environment.

Some people argue that there are actual conflicts among the major environmental laws. The General Accounting Office (GAO 1997a, p. 11) reports that "…differences in the requirements of the numerous planning and environmental laws…produce inefficiency and ineffectiveness in the Forest Service's decision-making. …differences between environmental laws and agencies' planning statutes can be difficult to reconcile." A 1992 Office of Technology Assessment report (OTA 1992, p. 59) on Forest Service planning notes,"The complex web of laws may make forest planning and activities slower, costlier, and less efficient than necessary to produce and protect the various resource values. Moreover, some laws guide the setting of management direction based on local conditions and public participation, while other laws establish requirements or standards for specific resources, values, or sites."

The problems arising from the web of statutes make it clear that federal land management policy must include strategies for dealing with statutory overlap. Making each agency responsible for enforcing the laws on its lands is one strategy. Another is to deal with overlaps through interagency agreements. Whatever the solution, the problem must be addressed.

Prescriptive versus nonprescriptive policies. Congress initially granted the executive resource management agencies broad discretion in defining and implementing multiple use and sustained yield as management concepts (Hagenstein 1992). In enacting MUSY, the Wilderness Act, NFMA, and FLPMA, Congress gradually retracted this authority from the executive agencies: with each new piece of legislation, the activities of the agencies have been incrementally constrained.

Throughout the more recent debates over federal land management, particularly on the national forests, Congress has faced the problem of how prescriptive its legislation should be. Early versions of bills considered during the debates leading up to passage of NFMA were prescriptive and would have written into law specific management direction for the national forests. The bill that ultimately formed the framework for NFMA was less prescriptive; it relied on planning to resolve management issues, thus permitting Forest Service professionals considerable room for discretion. In its final form, NFMA reflected the reluctance of Congress to impose management direction in law and legislators' historical trust of Forest Service professionals, yet at the same time Congress recognized the need for public involvement in the planning process.

The importance of prescriptive versus nonprescriptive legislative approaches should not be underestimated. At the time NFMA passed, one of the most important issues to foresters was preserving professional discretion in management. Shortly after its passage, James Giltmier, then a staff member on the Senate Committee on Agriculture and Forestry, wrote about the decision flexibility extended to the Forest Service under NFMA (Behan 1978):

> Failure in this mission will certainly mean that more legislation will come down the pipe at a later time, and when it does it will be prescriptive as hell.

Giltmier's prediction seems to have come true. For a variety of reasons, recent legislative and administrative proposals are more prescriptive than they have been in the past. For example, professional resource managers point out that the guidelines for implementing the president's Northwest Forest Plan (Tuchman et al. 1996) were highly prescriptive and constrained their flexibility.

A comparison of the statutes illustrates their increasingly detailed prescription. The 1897 Organic Act required one paragraph; MUSY, 1960, is two pages long; NFMA, 1976, runs 15 pages. The proposed Public Lands Management Improvement Act is 75 pages.

The General Accounting Office (GAO 1996) notes that the national forests are increasingly being managed for special purposes, such as wilderness, wild and scenic rivers, and recreation. In western Washington, Oregon, and California, for example, 77 percent of the 24.5 million acres of federal land that was available for commercial harvest has been set aside or withdrawn for primarily noncommodity uses. And although the remaining 5.5 million acres is available for regulated harvest, minimum requirements for maintaining biological diversity under NFMA, as well as air and water quality under the Clean Air and Clean Water Acts, respectively, may limit the timing, location, and amount of harvesting that can occur. Harvests from these lands could be further reduced by plans to protect threatened and endangered salmon.

The legislative environment is more complex than ever. Each of the laws has attempted to reconcile and harmonize federal land management with successive generations of environmental and other law. Additionally, Congress has slowly withdrawn its original broad grant of authority to the agencies. Some interest groups and many members of Congress believe that leaving management to the discretion of professionals has either failed to resolve the underlying problems or resulted in large-scale abuses of both the land and the law.

Financing land management. Many of the issues previously discussed are partly the result of insufficient or inappropriate allocation of funds among resources and regions. Insufficient funding to do the necessary tasks is a common problem for organizations, including federal agencies. Despite, or perhaps because of, the agreement to balance the federal budget, the current period of fiscal austerity seems likely to persist.

For agencies that sell or lease natural resources, one apparent solution is self-financing—paying for operations and investments from the revenues of those sales or leases. Although self-financing doesn't help meet federal budget targets (because reductions in revenues to the US Treasury must be offset by higher taxes or deficit spending), it does provide the federal land management agencies with an advantage over such agencies as Defense and Commerce, which do not have products or services to sell.

Is self-financing feasible? To assess this question, one must examine the extent to which the Forest Service and BLM are currently self-financed, then estimate the amount of revenue returned to the general treasury that might be retained. In federal budgeting, the most common phrase that identifies self-financing is "permanently appropriated funds," although "mandatory spending" and "indefinite appropriations" are also used. Congress has specifically authorized each permanent appropriation, usually in the statutes that created the trust fund or special account. Permanently appropriated accounts allow the agencies to spend the money that had been deposited in those accounts, in accordance with the authorizing statute, without any further action by Congress. In contrast, so-called discretionary appropriations must be enacted annually, prior to the beginning of the fiscal year, before the agencies can spend the money.[1]

Some trust funds and special accounts have been created without permanent appropriations and require annual appropriations. For the federal land management agencies, the two best-known special accounts that require annual appropriations are the Range Betterment Fund and the Land and Water Conservation Fund. The Range Betterment Fund was created by §401(b) of FLPMA with a credit of 50 percent of grazing fees from most western federal lands for subsequent use on range improvement activities. In the law, Congress authorized certain use of the funds but did not permanently appropriate the funds. Instead, each year the agencies must request that Congress appropriate the funds; Congress has consistently made available the full amount requested.

This contrasts with the Land and Water Conservation Fund, which was

---

[1] In some years (and with increasing frequency, it seems) Congress enacts one (or more) "continuing resolution" to fund the agencies temporarily, while it completes the work of enacting the annual appropriation bills.

created in 1964, partly to fund land acquisition for the federal land management agencies. It is credited with deposits from federal recreation user fees and motorboat fuel taxes, sales of surplus federal lands, and outer continental shelf oil and gas leases, up to $900 million annually. Congressional appropriations from the fund have almost never reached the amount deposited and declined to less than $140 million in fiscal year 1996. As a result, the Land and Water Conservation Fund has an unappropriated balance of more than $12 billion. This is not real money sitting in a special account waiting to be spent, however. The "credited deposits" are merely accounting entries that indicate how much Congress has authorized itself to spend from the account, and the "balance" is just the accumulated unappropriated authorized level of funding. Congress must still appropriate the funds to be spent from the Land and Water Conservation Fund annually in the Department of the Interior and Related Agencies Appropriations Act, and the agencies cannot spend more than Congress appropriates.

The Forest Service currently has 14 permanently appropriated trust funds and special accounts. Some of these (four in fiscal year 1996) are relatively modest, involving less than $5 million annually, but others are substantial: three exceed $100 million annually and another four, $10 million to $100 million annually. In total, the accounts provided $747 million of spending authority for the Forest Service in fiscal year 1996, compared with $2.479 billion of spending authority in annual appropriations. Thus, self-financing generated 23 percent of total Forest Service spending that year.

Total Forest Service receipts in fiscal year 1996 were $693 million; the Departments of Energy and the Interior collected another $171 million for mineral and energy activities in the national forests (USDA-FS 1996). Of the $864 million received, $412 million was deposited directly into various trust funds and special accounts, and $281 million was available for the payments to states and to counties and for the purchaser-elect timber roads. These accounts had total payments of $261 million in 1996, leaving $13 million to be deposited in the US Treasury.

Unless the Forest Service is allowed to use the revenues collected by other federal agencies from its forests, it cannot become self-financed.

Self-financing is a complex proposition for BLM as well. The agency has 18 permanently appropriated accounts that provided $96 million of spending authority for BLM in fiscal year 1996, compared with $1.106 billion of spending authority in annual appropriations. Thus, self-financing generated only 8 percent of total BLM spending that year.

Total BLM receipts in fiscal year 1996 were $147 million (USDI-BLM

1996). However, BLM lands also generate substantial mineral revenues that are collected by another Interior agency, the Minerals Management Service. In 1996 this agency's collections from BLM lands totaled $1.038 billion (USDI-MMS). Of the $147 million collected by BLM, $17 million was deposited directly into various trust funds and special accounts, leaving $130 million to cover the $78 million of payments to state and local governments. If the difference ($52 million) were available to increase BLM self-financing, it would cover only a small portion of BLM's $1.106 billion budget. But if BLM programs could be financed from the mineral revenues currently collected by the Minerals Management Service, the agency would be virtually self-financing at current operating levels.

BLM thus has the potential to become self-financing. For the Forest Service—and for BLM as well, if using mineral revenues proves politically infeasible—there are only two routes toward self-financing: higher revenues and lower costs.

Increasing revenues. Expanding or even maximizing revenues to increase self-financing is a possibility.[2] Markets, for example, could be used to allocate resources among users. Markets are currently used only for timber and certain minerals (defined by law as leasable minerals). Other resources—rangeland, hardrock and common minerals, developed and dispersed recreation uses, and other special uses—are sold at administered (rather than market) prices, generally set by law or regulation. Raising fees for such uses to fair market values might significantly increase agency revenues. Even for currently marketed resources, expanded use of marketing practices may enhance revenues.

Proponents of markets have asserted that some resource values could be enhanced through markets. Management to enhance or protect water quality for municipal water supplies or to develop recreational opportunities, for example, would arguably be expanded if the agencies received significant revenues from these efforts (see O'Toole 1988). However, other resource values—especially those that cannot be marketed—might be devalued or physically degraded. For example, protecting nongame bird habitat or recovering endangered species would become constraints on management, rather than goals to be achieved through management. Future values (and the productivity of the land) might also be compro-

---

[2] It is commonly thought that the legal definition of multiple use (in MUSY for the Forest Service and in FLPMA for the BLM) prohibits the agencies from managing to maximize revenues. The law allows them not to maximize revenues but does not prohibit such management: "…with consideration being given to the relative values of the various resources, and not ncessarily the combination that will give the greatest dollar return or the greatest unit output."

mised. For example, high-graded timber stands, from which many of the best trees have been removed, might result from efforts to maximize current timber revenues.

Other means of increasing revenues include selling or leasing federal land. Some federal lands, because of their location, have significant market values. The Forest Service and BLM administer lands adjacent to many towns, especially in the West. The sale of modest amounts of land with commercial value as residential or industrial sites could raise significant sums for land management.

However, federal land sales are frequently opposed for a variety of reasons. For example, sites with access to a lake would likely have considerable market value for vacation homes, but their sale would reduce public opportunities to use and share such sites by concentrating access in the hands of those wealthy enough to acquire them. Even where these sites are leased under the Summer Homes Program, they are undervalued and do not generate market-driven revenues. Another reason for opposition to federal land sales is that selling assets to generate revenues to cover operating costs is a poor business practice, one that can ultimately lead to bankruptcy. It is uncertain whether legislative land sale authority could be written with sufficient precision to encourage the sale of sites with low value for resource management (including recreational use) but high commercial value, while preventing the sale of sites with high value for resource management.

Reducing costs. Lower operating costs would obviously improve the prospects for self-financing. Innumerable studies, by groups both internal and external to the agencies, have attempted to identify new, lower-cost ways of doing business. Studies have examined and recommended changes in organizational structures; monitoring and incentives; production processes, such as timber sale practices and contracting; and budgeting and accounting practices, including trust funds and special accounts (Liggett et al. 1995, p. 157-83).

A significant difficulty with decreasing costs is that many of the options for improving efficiency have enormous ramifications—for the lands and resources, for agency personnel, and for the various users and other interests—that extend far beyond "simple" changes that improve efficiency. In addition, the individuals and interest groups most concerned about the national forests and public lands have historically not argued for efficiency in federal land management.

Legislative or administrative changes that significantly improve the efficiency of federal land management seem unlikely without becoming intertwined in the larger policy debates about the purposes of federal land management. The inevitable conclusion is that increasing self-financing by improving efficiency is unlikely without other substantial legislative or administrative changes in the agencies' management.

Interagency and Regulatory Issues

A third set of issues deals with interagency coordination and administrative and regulatory issues that affect national forest and public land management.

Appeals and litigation.[3] The Forest Service and BLM each have a different system of administrative appeals for agency land management decisions. FLPMA directs the secretary of Interior to "structure adjudication procedures to assure adequate third party participation, objective administrative review of initial decisions, and expeditious decision making" (43 U.S.C. §1701(a)(5)). NFMA does not contain similar express language but does require public participation, especially for the development of forest plans. The statutes do not specifically address judicial review; neither statute contains citizen suit provisions. Therefore, judicial review is available as authorized in the Administrative Procedure Act.

Agency responses to appeals are often different. The Forest Service usually stays a project while the appeal is being reviewed; BLM typically does not. If a BLM project is protested and the deciding official believes the protest has no merit, the sale will be offered, but award of the sale is delayed 45 days to allow the protesters to request a stay.

Forest Service appeals. Forest Service regulations provide for three types of administrative appeals: 36 C.F.R. Part 215 regulations govern appeals of most projects and activities, such as timber sales; 36 C.F.R. Part 217 regulations govern appeals of forest plans, standards, and guidelines; and 36 C.F.R. Part 251 regulations govern appeals of permits and other actions involving particular persons doing business in the forest or using forest lands. The number of appeals originating under each set of regulations varies greatly. In fiscal year 1996, of the 1,089 pending appeals, 882 were Part 215 (project) appeals, 31 were Part 217 (plan) appeals, and 163 were Part 251 (permit) appeals.

The cost of the appeals process is significant. Hill (1997) estimated the cost of managing the 1996 appeals at approximately $7 million.

Much of the recent controversy concerns timber sales. Baldwin (1997)

---

[3] Much of this discussion is drawn from Baldwin 1997. Federal land management: Appeals and litigation. Overview prepared for a workshop held by the Senate Committee on Energy and Natural Resources, February 26. Washington, DC: Congressional Research Service.

reports that in fiscal year 1996 there were 1,035 potentially appealable timber sales. There were an additional 3,612 sales that were not appealable, principally because of the salvage rider limitations. Of the timber sales that were potentially appealable, 148 (14 percent) were appealed, and 45 sales were withdrawn by the Forest Service as a result, removing 58 million board feet of timber from offer.

The purpose of administrative appeals is to provide an avenue of redress for citizens dissatisfied with agency decisions. Typically, administrative appeals are far less costly than lawsuits. In fiscal year 1996, when 1,089 administrative appeals were pending, the USDA's Office of General Counsel estimated that 100 lawsuits involved forest plans and implementing activities.

Bureau of Land Management protests. Citizens can protest a BLM management decision to the deciding official. The protest may be accepted and the decision changed, or the protest may be rejected. If the protest is rejected, the decision becomes appealable to the Interior Board of Land Appeals.

However, timber management cases represent only a small portion of all BLM administrative appeals. In fact, between fiscal years 1992 and 1996, the board disposed of only 71 BLM timber management cases.

Since some protests of BLM managers' decisions bypass the board of appeals and proceed directly to court, the number of timber sales litigated is also relevant. No official figures are available, but BLM estimates that over the past five years, three cases have been brought against resource management plans, and seven cases involve implementation. Some decisions are made directly by the secretary and are not subject to the administrative appeals process. Decisions at this level are the exception and are occasionally used to expedite implementation.

Amending the appeals process. Opinions on the appeals process abound. Some argue that appeals provide an essential avenue for meaningful public participation in the management of the federal lands; that appeals have helped compel the agencies to follow the laws more closely; and that the appeals procedures can be improved. Critics assert that the number of appeals stymies land management by these agencies; that many appeals are frivolous or motivated by the desire to delay land management rather than to improve it; and that the resulting costs are exorbitant. Proposals to address these contentions generally seek to limit when and where appeals can be filed, who can file appeals, and what is appealable.

Some proposals call for shortening the time potential appellants have to initiate administrative appeals. These limitations generally vary with the complexity of the management decision: the more complex, the more time allowed. This proposal might have two effects. It could expedite agency actions, but it could also preclude justifiable appeals that prevent the implementation of unwise or harmful agency actions or increase litigation.

Other proposals limit who may file appeals so that parties who were never involved in the public participation process cannot "ambush" the agency. Generally, these proposals limit standing to challenge agency decisions to those who have commented on the issue for which they seek administrative review. Standing has been long established as a legitimate legal device, and it does not necessarily limit legitimate participation in government; still, the approach raises broad questions about the purposes and scope of public participation in government.

Tougher sanctions for frivolous appeals have received widespread attention and support. Baldwin (1997) reports that appeal-deciding officers may dismiss an appeal without review for various reasons, but Forest Service regulations do not mention "frivolous" appeals. In fiscal year 1996 the Forest Service dismissed 230 administrative appeals on various grounds, including 16 for lack of content and 165 for lack of standing.

In addition to the regulations on administrative appeals, Baldwin reports there are currently rules for dismissal of frivolous lawsuits. The Federal Rules of Civil Procedure provide for sanctions against attorneys and clients who file suits that are not well grounded in fact, existing law, and good-faith argument. Such grounds for dismissal have not been readily used, however.

Jurisdictional requirements have also been proposed, to limit where judicial appeals can be filed. Specific types of appeals would have to be filed in appellate courts, to shorten the time required to finalize and implement management decisions.

Public participation. Involving the public in federal decisionmaking became an important issue in the late 1960s and early 1970s. The trend cut across all fields of public policy, not just natural resources management.

Requirements for public involvement in land management planning were specifically included in NFMA, together with a requirement that Forest Service plans and revisions be made available to the public "at convenient locations in the vicinity of the affected unit" (Sec. 6(d)). Public participation had been long established in the Bureau of Land Management through advisory committees established under the Taylor Grazing Act.

The regulations implementing NFMA, and their subsequent revisions, included specific guidance on how public involvement was to be achieved. In addition, MUSY provided a theoretical framework for public participation through its focus on multiple-use resource management. Regulations implementing the National Environmental Policy Act provide for substantial public involvement in federal decisionmaking.

Forest Service implementation of NFMA's public participation requirements has been uneven—occasionally effective, but more often not. These legal requirements of NFMA are not substantive; at best they are vague and imprecise. Consequently, they have often led to planning actions that have failed to meet the expectations of some interest groups. The model used by the agencies seeks to inform and educate, on the assumption that if citizens "understand" what the agency is going to do, they will accept those actions. In many cases, public participation has been used to seek public acceptance, rather than to truly involve the public in crafting management options.

Several high-profile cases exemplify how empowering the public has changed the dynamics of the planning process. Among them is the Quincy Library Group. Here, citizens representing the timber industry, local government, and environmental concerns in northern California developed a proposal for forest management on the Plumas and Lassen National Forests and the Sierraville Ranger District of the Tahoe National Forest. The proposal attempts to create a future forest condition (an all-age, multistory, fire-resilient forest) acceptable to all parties. The agreement was heralded as a success for community-based planning, but problems emerged when the group sought implementation: the initial authorizing legislation failed but was later included in the fiscal year 1999 appropriations bill. Legislative approval of community-level decisionmaking is problematic. Formal sanction of such proposals by legislatures opens the decision to broader interest-group influence that is usually not present or is configured differently at a smaller spatial scale (Goergen et al. 1997).

Rather than resolving the underlying issues, the current system tends to provide a forum for localizing the struggle among competing interests. Changing the spatial scale of the planning and public involvement process provides tactical advantages and disadvantages for the various interests, often leading to charges that one side or the other "bargained in bad faith" and then resorted to judicial proceedings to win its case.

The role of public involvement (and the spatial and temporal scales for their involvement) in natural resources planning must be clarified by changes in the law, implementing regulations, and practice. Until that occurs, it is unlikely that a planning process will help resolve the underlying conflicts.

Community stability and change. A report of the Society of American

Foresters (SAF 1989) includes the following ideas about community stability among its conclusions and recommendations:

• Global social and economic change is a fact of life over which local communities and the forestry profession have extremely limited influence. There are, however, ways that communities can influence their own destinies. The question is how effectively individual communities will adjust to macrolevel change.

• The ability to engage in orderly change depends on what a community chooses to do with available resources, both physical and human. Public agencies and private organizations can destabilize communities by creating conditions of uncertainty or abruptly changing (particularly reducing) the availability of resources on which a community has relied. Predictability is vital for community adaptability; excessive and prolonged uncertainty leads to disorganization and maladaptation.

The interests of communities and the industries on which they depend are not always the same. Certainly the interests of communities and industries can and do coincide in many instances, but there is generally a clear distinction between industrial stability and community stability—a distinction too often overlooked.

State, local, and tribal government interests. The Office of Technology Assessment's 1992 report on forest planning (OTA 1992, p. 105–6) provides a succinct summary of the jurisdiction issues in federal land management:

> State, tribal, and local governments have particular interests in national forest planning and management. States have jurisdiction over and responsibility for certain resources, such as water rights and fish and wildlife management, and the laws governing Forest Service planning and decisionmaking preserve these State Rights. Furthermore, many States regulate forest management practices, at least on State and private lands. Thus cooperation between the Forest Service and the relevant State agencies is an important part of national forest planning.

MUSY and NFMA require the Forest Service to cooperate with state and other government agencies. However, cooperation does not provide the states or other governments with legal leverage to influence plans or decisions. Coordinated state responses to Forest Service plans and decisions are more likely to be influential than independent agency responses.

State and local governments have a poorly defined role but an important interest in federal land management planning. Maintaining their economies and sustaining ecosystems are priorities. These governments represent particular interests, and coordination among the various landowners is necessary to sustain ecosystems. States, through their forest practice regulations and their state forest resource planning, have knowledge and expertise in coordinating management of multiple landowners.

Federal land and state, tribal, and private lands are often intermixed. This raises the question of access across federal lands—something that has not been addressed consistently or efficiently. The issue of access should be addressed so that nonfederal landowners have a clear understanding of the process and their rights and responsibilities.

Because states are responsible for air and water quality standards under the Clean Air and Clean Water Acts, federal agencies must comply with state standards. Enforcement of these standards has led to disagreements over fire management and the cumulative impacts of forest management on water quality. Although the state governments have traditionally had responsibility for wildlife and fisheries management, the Endangered Species Act, the Sikes Act, and other statutes have considerably broadened the role of the federal government in fish and wildlife management.

Revenue sharing with the Forest Service and BLM under several programs has provided local governments with a direct financial interest in the management of public lands. The current system of revenue sharing pays various percentages of gross receipts to the counties where the commodities are produced. In addition to revenue sharing, the federal government also provides payment in lieu of taxes to many local governments. In some cases transfers have been made between state and federal governments for management of wildlife habitat on federal lands.

A less obvious example of the revenue impacts on state governments is the result of federal decisions for wildlife habitat management. In some states, substantial revenue is raised through licenses for fishing and hunting, particularly big game. License sales and huntable populations are largely determined through cooperative management of federal lands by state and federal wildlife managers.

Intergovernmental relations reveal many of the same complexities as nested ecosystems. The differing spatial scales of state, local, and tribal governments and differences in political culture and values often lead directly to differing concerns about federal land management. Federal lands dominate many counties and some states in the West. That domination often leads to significant concern for the economic and social viability of the communities located within these public lands.

Biodiversity. Biological diversity has become one of the most contentious issues in forest planning. The Society of American Foresters (SAF 1997) defines biological diversity as the variety and abundance of species, their genetic composition, and the communities, ecosystems, and landscapes in which they occur. The term also refers to ecological structures, functions, and processes at all of these levels. Biological diversity occurs at spatial scales that range from local to regional to global.

Biological diversity became an issue in federal land management during the debate on NFMA. What was originally a discussion of concerns over type conversions (converting native oak-hickory stands to pine plantations in the South) was translated into the diversity provision (Sec. 6(g)(3)(b)) of NFMA. This section, which combines language from the House and the Senate, provides open-ended, unclear direction on dealing with diversity. Although more explicit, the implementing regulations for forest planning still leave a great deal to interpretation and considerable opportunity for planners to exercise discretion in meeting this requirement. Consequently, they invite administrative and legal appeals of forest plans on grounds of failure to meet the intent or spirit of the diversity requirement.

An Office of Technology Assessment report (OTA 1992) summarizes a number of studies of implementing the diversity requirements in forest planning. One point is clear: no national forest had data that would constitute a satisfactory basis on which to develop plans to "provide for diversity," as the law requires. The measures of diversity most commonly used in forest plans are timber or range vegetation types and different age classes of forest or range types. One study cited in the report concluded that although plans for the 20 forests studied "generally conformed with NFMA requirements to provide for diversity and show effects of outputs on diversity, the measures of diversity were general values for tree age classes or animal numbers, rather than specific measures for plant and animal communities and species distribution and abundance." Several forest plans even proposed conversions to monocultures of nonnative species, artificial planting with pine, and extensive habitat fragmentation—practices that would not protect biological resources.

Because the diversity provision has been a basis for disputes over old-growth management and a lightning rod for many appeals of forest plans, it is not surprising that the newest draft of the planning regulations features a much-expanded treatment of the subject. Nevertheless, this draft omits a section on species viability, which is a key component of the current regulations and earlier drafts of the revised regulations. Clarifying the intent of the diversity provision and translating that intent into planning practice are among the most urgent issues facing the national forests.

No such provisions concerning biodiversity appear in any BLM statutes or regulations. Nonetheless, the issues involved in managing for diversity are as important on BLM lands as they are on those of the Forest Service, and the need for clarifying legislative direction extends to all of the federal lands.

As a Society of American Foresters report on forest health and productivity noted, the concept of forest health is loosely defined and is often most relevant to the beholder (SAF 1993). There is no doubt, however, that many of the nation's forests, both public and private, are in some stage of recovery from human disturbance. On the national forests in particular, there are many young dense stands with associated fire, insect, and disease problems. Recovery is a long-term process that requires significant financial investment, patience, and new knowledge. Forest management can assist in the restoration of forest health, and professional natural resource managers have an important role to play in this activity.

An emerging approach to managing for biodiversity may reduce the need for "crisis" responses to declining species. The coarse filter–fine filter approach (Carrol et al. 1996) is based on the finding that consistent groups of animal and plant species are commonly found associated with each other and dependent on certain forest conditions. These conditions are often stand structures or combinations of structures within a forest type. Different species associations can depend on mutually exclusive structures; for example, some species depend on openings and others on complex forests. Some species also depend on very specific conditions within a structure; for example, some bat species may need large hollow cavities or deeply furrowed bark within the complex structure. Coarse-filter management is a metaphor for maintaining enough of each characteristic structure within the forest area so that most species survive. If some species—for example, the bats that require deeply furrowed bark— are still endangered because they need specific conditions not provided within a structure, they are then individually addressed with more specific habitat provisions. The current Endangered Species Act provides only a fine-filter approach. Efforts to protect habitats needed by endangered species can cause habitats needed by other species to disappear from the landscape. By adding a coarse filter of all structures on each forest type, many species could be kept from becoming endangered.

Agency accountability, public confidence, and performance. Gaining the confidence and support of the people served by an agency is an important goal of all public organizations. Gifford Pinchot composed the original mission statement for the Forest Service in a letter that he drafted for James Wilson, under-secretary of Agriculture, in 1906 (Dana 1956, p. 142–43). The national forests, he wrote, are to be managed "from the standpoint of the greatest good of the greatest number in the long run." This paraphrase of English utilitarian philosopher Jeremy Bentham (de Steiguer 1994) captures the idealism of conservation as envisioned by the Progressives at the beginning of the 20th century. Through the early

1960s, the Forest Service had a reputation for being one of the most efficient and effective federal agencies (Kaufman 1960). This reputation has
tarnished as public demands have changed.

A recent General Accounting Office report (GAO 1997a, p. 6) suggests
that the Forest Service has "not given adequate attention to reducing the
costs and time of its decisionmaking process and improving its ability to
deliver what is expected or promised." The report was particularly critical of the agency's monitoring program, noting that it does "not adequately monitor the effects of past management decisions ... maintain
comparable environmental and socioeconomic data ... [or] adequately involve the public at the beginning of the decision-making process."

Monitoring has been a traditionally difficult issue in natural resources
management. It is expensive to do, and veteran resource managers are
often frustrated because the data collected are often ignored in the politically charged atmosphere of public decisionmaking. The data can also
provide ammunition to those who would seek to overturn a decision because the agency inaccurately predicted its results.

This report cannot replicate the scope and detail of the cited Government Accounting Office report. Concerned readers should study it carefully but also consider that during 1998, the Forest Service undertook important changes in its administrative structure and made public commitments to improving agency accountability.

Scale of analysis. The scale of analysis refers to the geographic area or
time span considered in planning. BLM has typically used resource areas
as the spatial scale. The Forest Service uses the national forest; the forest
boundaries have been based on a combination of political and resource
criteria, which may or may not be the best scale for analysis. The two-level
decision process used by the Forest Service under NFMA first considered
all the resources and values in a congressionally designated national forest, followed by an implementation decision under NEPA that considered
all of the information in the project area.

There have been suggestions for changes to the scale used. One suggestion is to make broad decisions at the province level and specific decisions at the watershed level. Another configuration could be political,
at the state level for broad decisions and at the county level for specific
decisions covered by NEPA. Or there could be any combination of levels,
using political, economic, or biologic and hydrologic boundaries. The
planning area could include public and private lands, not just Forest Service or BLM lands. Including private lands would help managers understand the condition of the private resource and its expected contributions to social well-being, then design land management plans and tech-

nical and financial assistance programs to achieve the desired results.

Another scale of planning refers to the time the plan is expected to endure. Under current regulations, the period is 15 years. Some critics have argued for a longer period, some for a shorter period, and some for maximizing the flexibility in the length of time for each plan.

Third-party certification of public lands. The basis for the international movement toward third-party certification of sustainable management and use of natural resources is that market forces and consumer behavior can be used to influence forest management and address environmental concerns. (A special report by the Society of American Foresters addressed the issue [SAF 1995], and a task force is updating that report and offering alternatives for SAF's role in certification.)

We will not elaborate the pros and cons of certification. Instead, we want to address the specific question of third-party certification as it may apply to Forest Service and BLM management.

A common theme among those advocating certification is that existing regulatory mechanisms are not fully in place (Elliott 1996). This argument, as applied to federal agencies, is difficult to accept. Both the Forest Service and BLM are subject to a plethora of laws and regulations that, in combination with the public participation process, are more stringent than any certification process being considered. In any case, more regulation and more planning will not necessarily improve public trust.

When considering certification of Forest Service and BLM practices, we must recognize the political aspects of the issues. Much of the opposition to public land management stems from differing values. Given the frequent shifts in public values and ideals, it would be difficult to create an objective certification process: there would be tremendous political pressure to have the certifying parties represent one set of values over another.

Citizens often want someone they trust to verify that good decisions are being made about their land and to assure them that their needs are being met. It may be that third-party certification or verification could address intense distrust of both government and industry. It could also be argued that the current planning process, which includes opportunity for administrative appeals and litigation, is itself a form of third-party certification.

3

Evaluating Federal Forest Policy and Decisionmaking

Because forestry is science based and value driven (Bentley 1995), natural resource professionals often attempt to apply the value-transparent approaches of science to the inherently value-laden field of public policy. Developing a set of universal criteria for evaluating natural resources policy and decisionmaking at the national, forest, and district levels is a challenge. Many authors have suggested broad models of the public policy process (see Jones 1984). There are also a variety of policy analysis and decision analysis tools and frameworks. For example, in their recent forest health report, Oliver et al. (1997) used a traditional matrix approach to classify management approaches and policy options.

One factor that complicates analytical frameworks is the ill-defined boundary between analyzing public policy and analyzing decisionmaking. Anderson (1984) describes decisionmaking as a component of policymaking. He writes: "Decision-making involves the choice of an alternative from among a series of competing alternatives. Policy-making typically involves a pattern of action, extending over time and involving many decisions." That is, an initiative to list a particular species or population as endangered or designate critical habitat is a *decision*. Passing a series of laws establishing and implementing the endangered species program is *policy*.

Alas, there is no bright line. Where the decision or policy is made is not often a useful indicator. The courts, legislature, and administrative agencies all make decisions and set policies—some broad in scope, some quite narrow. One might reasonably argue that the forest planning process constitutes a series or pattern of actions and therefore represents policy. Others examine the same circumstances and see a decision. Is the plan a decision or a precursor to management? The courts, agencies, and interest groups remain divided.

We have adapted a set of criteria by which we can evaluate several pending legislative proposals for the national forests and public lands. The criteria reflect both a broad approach to policy analysis and a narrow focus on decision analysis. We believe the following criteria should prove useful for analysis of proposed legislation and management plans.

Policy Analysis

Clawson (1975) authored one of the most widely used sets of criteria for evaluating public policy after participating in the President's Advisory Panel on Timber and the Environment from 1971 to 1973. More than 25 years later, his framework of analysis for forest policy still has much to offer both professional policy analysts and natural resource specialists. It is simple enough to be easily communicated, and it is comprehensive. As Clawson points out, however, the criteria are interrelated, and some are not easily separated. Briefly stated, Clawson's criteria are as follows.

Physical and biological feasibility and consequences. Clawson writes that one can be fairly certain that there will be major differences of opinion on the "facts" in nearly all forest policy controversies because of the tremendous variability of forests, our incomplete knowledge of forest science, and the necessity of predicting the likely outcome of a proposed policy. Nonetheless, it is important to establish the areas of agreement among the participants early in the process.

Economic efficiency. Analyzing the costs and benefits of a proposed policy is as much art as science—perhaps more. Many assumptions must be made, and market values for many of the amenities and products produced by forested ecosystems are lacking. Yet the analysis of cost effectiveness continues to be a powerful tool.

Economic welfare or equity. Clawson observed that the economic benefits of a program of forest management accrue to certain individuals or groups, and the costs fall on other individuals or groups. "Only rarely, if ever, will the two groups be identical in composition and will the production of benefits and costs be exactly equal." It is probably easier to estimate gains or losses in economic efficiency than in equity. Clawson asks, "...do the users of the wilderness or recreationists have a more legitimate claim to the benefits of the forest ...than the city residents whose houses might cost less if the timber were harvested? The answer to such questions obviously involves one's personal value system..."

Social or cultural acceptability. Social choices are guided by the goals, ideals, and aspirations that arise from personal and community values systems—particularly in federal and state forestry, where policies are set through a complex, deliberative public process. "Those who are offended by large areas of clearcut timber, and/or by large volumes of low-grade or rotting logs left behind," Clawson wrote, "...are not mollified by evidence that such methods of timber harvest may have been economically efficient or silviculturally desirable."

Operational or administrative practicality. A forest policy must be operationally and administratively practical if it is to be successful. The administering organization must have decisionmakers who recognize and consider the issues and can gather and consider reasonable amounts of information. In addition, they must be able to translate general decisions into specific actions and provide continuing supervision and feedback.

Those criteria are interdependent and cannot be simultaneously maximized. Some criteria will be considered more important than others by the interest groups and institutions involved. In the political process, the most likely outcome will be the result of structured compromises among those most interested in the decision.

Decision Analysis

The public participation process provides an opportunity to constructively evaluate public land management plans and decisions. The following criteria for decision analysis are derived from an extensive review of the forest management and systems literature. It is one of several approaches that might be used to systematically analyze complex land management decisions.

1. Identifying Goals and Objectives

Purpose. The initial stages of decision analysis are often the most important and difficult to accomplish. The purpose for making the decision should be explicit.

Values and concerns. The values and concerns of the interested and affected parties should be clarified. This step is often complicated because many parties may be involved and because values are complex constructs that change over time and in relation to the issues under scrutiny. In public land management, it is unlikely that all the parties will agree on a common set of values. It is important to identify all the values, including the values of the members or units providing the decision analysis.

2. Developing Alternatives

Baseline inventories. Resource inventories are a critical starting point for decisionmaking. Inventory data must originate on the ground, generally at the lowest spatial scale by the lowest organizational level. The data must retain their spatial integrity for decisions at the lowest levels but also permit aggregation for baseline information at other organizational levels. What is inventoried must be revised periodically to reflect changes in scientific knowledge and social values.

Because inventories are expensive to develop and maintain, however, they must provide information that is relevant and appropriate. The technologies of data collection, moreover, can generate false data—the appearance of accuracy, because computer data look authoritative—or create an incomplete picture.

Open-ended process. The options should include the extremes and apparently risky choices. Alternatives that violate earlier, higher-level decisions, such as existing resource management plans and even current laws, should be examined so that the consequences of retaining or changing those decisions can be seen.

Because analyses can sometimes identify new or unusual combinations of alternatives, the list should not be considered complete until the decision is made. The goal is to find an option that provides more desired values at less cost or damage (including declines in other values).

Alternatives result only from discussion and dissent. Dissent broadens the understanding of the problem; disagreement provides real alternatives and stimulates new and different ways of perceiving and understanding (Drucker 1974). Thus, discussion and dissent, though uncomfortable for many of us, lead to a full array of alternatives—a necessary condition for effective decisionmaking.

3. Analyzing Alternatives

Analysis of the likely and possible consequences of alternatives is an important part of the decisionmaking process. The summary and conclusions from analyses must be presented coherently, and the limitations of the analysis must be expressed. Succinct presentations of alternatives and their likely consequences are essential.

Thoroughness. Analyzing alternatives should result in the best estimate, or a range of most likely estimates, of the expected consequences of the choices. Analyses need to cover all the relevant resources and effects (on-site and off-site) of a proposed plan or action. Although an alternative might address one issue or value (e.g., preserving roadless areas), the analysis of that alternative must display the best estimates of the consequences on all the values and concerns. Reporting on the full range of expected consequences allows the public and the decisionmakers to make an informed choice and provides the basis for monitoring the results.

Openness. Scientists in other parts of the agency, in other federal and nonfederal agencies, in academia, and in interest groups often have useful data, information, and analytical tools. Access to such support is through public review, including public peer review, which can spot errors, ignorance, and bias. Decisionmakers must be careful to include the public in the analytical process so that citizens can understand the complexity of the trade-offs and the variability of the estimates.

Documentation of the models and assumptions used in the analysis allows the public and peer reviewers to determine the validity of the estimates, or to explain why they believe the estimates erroneous.

Appropriateness. Analyses can always be improved through better information and better tools, but such improvements cost time and money. Sometimes the costs are warranted, but delays also have a price.

Because forests are dynamic and subject to seral, evolutionary, and catastrophic changes, delays can render decisions moot or alternatives irrelevant. Time periods for development and analysis should therefore be set at the outset, and the resources invested in developing and analyzing alternatives need to be commensurate with the values at stake, including the agency outlays, costs to users, and environmental consequences caused by delay.

The spatial and temporal scales used for analysis must also be appropriate for the decision. There should be sufficient detail on the alternatives and their expected consequences—but not excessive detail. For example, in land and resource management planning, an analysis of the estimated impact of each alternative on every plant and animal population potentially existing within the planning area would be so voluminous that the impacts on critical species might get lost. On the other hand, a finding that some species will survive better than others would be so simplistic as to be useless. The appropriate level of detail is commensurate with the values at risk and the capacity of the human mind.

4. Deciding and Implementing

Decisions are choices among options, not choices between right and wrong, good and evil. There are no guaranteed solutions, and risk is inherent in the process because the decision commits current resources to an uncertain and unknowable future.

Sometimes a compromise is a feasible alternative. In other situations, compromise might be the worst possible choice—if, for example, reducing timber harvesting levels might cause economic and social disruption while only postponing the extirpation of an endangered species.

It is not a tautology to note that decisions must be made by the decisionmaker. Affected and interested individuals and groups want to influence the decision and are involved in the analysis, but ultimately, the decisionmaker—not the computer models, expert systems, and other decision support tools—is responsible. And the decisionmaker must be able to change course when results indicate that the original decision was ineffective or inappropriate.

Timeliness. Decisionmakers sometimes postpone making decisions even though the analyses are complete. Delays can be costly, however, and deadlines for decisions should therefore be set and met unless extraordinary circumstances warrant.

Decentralization. The individuals who are most responsible for the environmental and economic consequences of the decisions should generally make decisions. Henri Fayol (1949) identified this matching of authority with responsibility as an important management principle nearly a century ago. "Responsible official," the term typically used in laws and other guides, is an appropriate designation for the decisionmaker.

The extent of others' involvement depends on several factors: the time available for a decision (whether an emergency exists or debate and deliberation are feasible), the extent of reversibility (how long it would take for the impacts to be substantially reversed); and the frequency of similar decisions (whether decisions like this are made weekly, monthly, annually, or once in a generation). In general, decisionmaking should be more collaborative when more time is available, reversibility is difficult, or the decision is infrequent (Drucker 1974).

Another factor is who will be affected by the expected consequences, including both those who will implement the decision and those who will live by it. Again, the more people affected by the decision, the more collaborative decisionmaking should generally be.

Transparency. The decision should be clear to those who must implement it, to those affected by or interested in it, and to higher officials who might review or be asked about it. This clarity can best be demonstrated by asking the six traditional questions:

Who made the decision, and who will implement it?

What was the problem or issue, and what decision was made?

When will the decision be implemented?

Where will the decision be implemented, and where can interested parties get more information?

Why was that alternative selected?

How was the decision made, and how will it be implemented?

The answers to those questions should be readily available to the various internal and external interests.

5. Monitoring the Results

Tracking. The decision must be trackable: it must identify the expected benefits, the expected outputs and other desirable results, and the expected costs, both economic and environmental. Standards for determining when the results fall short of the expectations should be established.

The decision document needs to specify the monitoring process and the modifications, mitigations, or revisions that will occur if standards are not met. All interested parties can then know the next steps if the results fall short of expectations. The monitoring process should include the following:

Who will do the monitoring?

What will be monitored?

When will the monitoring occur?

Where will the monitoring occur?

Why will monitoring occur?

How will the monitoring be accomplished (and funded)?

Timeliness. Monitoring should be timely to minimize the consequences of decisions that turn out to cause major problems, yet it should not interfere with implementation. The trade-offs are discussed thoroughly by Drucker (1974) in the context of continuous monitoring by business. Balancing the need to check performance with the response rates of natural systems is an art, not a science. Some time is required for the consequences to appear, but too long a delay in monitoring can lead to significant, unforeseen impacts.

Meaningfulness. Monitoring must be meaningful: it must evaluate performance in achieving the goals and objectives identified at the outset of the decisionmaking process. Although the measurements can be scientific, the goals may not be easily quantifiable. How, for example, can solitude be monitored with data on average wilderness use if visitors are not uniformly distributed? Quantitative measures, and complex computer models in particular, can give a false sense of accuracy. Assessing the validity of the assumptions and other inputs to computer models and other projections can be also be achieved through monitoring, but such validation monitoring differs from monitoring performance (implementation monitoring and effectiveness monitoring) (see OTA 1992).

For some values, a quantifiable proxy might prove acceptable; for example, stream turbidity might be an adequate measure of the quality of salmon spawning habitat. The public must agree that the measures are appropriate for the value. When appropriate quantitative measures simply don't exist, the opinions of the affected individuals and groups may be the only way—and for public land managers, ultimately the most important way—to assess performance.

Cost-effectiveness. Monitoring can almost always be improved through more and better measurement. But the time and money spent on monitoring must be commensurate with the values at stake and weighed against the potential costs of delayed feedback.

4

Recommendations

Conflict over public land policy and management is an enduring theme in American history (Dana 1956). The Pine Tree Riot in 1772, when the king's sheriff was terrorized by a band of timber thieves; the Land Ordinance of 1785, when the states yielded their land claims to the new federal government; the commotion that attended the creation of the forest reserves in 1891 (Steen 1997); intergovernmental competition for control of the public lands in the 20th century; sporadic incidents of arson by people protesting public acquisition and proposed management: such examples illustrate the violence, disagreement, and lack of consensus that mark the history of US public land policy. History provides little reason to believe that these fundamental differences will be resolved in the near future as a result of legislative and regulatory proposals now before Congress and the president. Nevertheless, new legislation seems the best approach for improving federal land management.

Revising the policies for managing the lands administered by the Forest Service and the Bureau of Land Management (BLM) is not a new idea. Debate over public land management has occurred many times in this country's past, and there have been periodic studies of the policies governing federal land management and of the structure through which those policies are delivered. The usual result has been not dramatic changes in direction but incremental change, with new policies laid on top of those already existing.

Incremental change in governance is the norm in the United States for several reasons, including the structure of the federal government, a general fear of large-scale change among citizens, and interest group activity that illustrates the conflicting values Americans hold for a variety of issues, including their public lands.

Public land managers increasingly operate in a politically charged environment. Interest is frequently pitted against interest, and meaningful agreements rarely seem to arise among the most deeply involved parties. A fundamental problem facing public resource managers is that the broad consensus that supports federal landownership and management is so diffuse that it frequently breaks down when applied to specific areas or issues. Arguments for transferring federal lands to the states or private owners have failed several times during the 20th century to attract sufficient support to make them politically viable. Yet there is little agreement among the interest groups about the purposes for which we should manage the national forests and public lands.

Foresters and ecologists understand that forests change over time. Sometimes the change takes centuries to occur, at other times it happens in a few violent minutes, but eventually one forest gives way to another. In the following pages we cultivate the seedlings of change, beginning with a summary of the reasons that change is needed.

• The purposes of the national forests and public lands are no longer clear. In the last two decades, changing public values, court decisions, administrative agendas, and federal environmental laws have combined to emphasize biodiversity, ecosystem functions and forest health on the national forests and public lands. The basic land management statutes have not been revised in more than 20 years and no longer adequately convey the public purposes or the priorities for which these lands should be managed.

• The management planning process for the national forests and public lands cannot resolve basic differences in values. In both the National Forest Management Act (NFMA) and the Federal Land Policy and Management Act (FLPMA), Congress assumed that a locally based, rational, and comprehensive planning process could resolve fundamental differences in values about public forests and rangelands. More than 20 years of agency experience, appeals, and lawsuits indicates this is not the case.

• Congress has never adequately defined the roles of local communities in implementing its broad legislative statements. Is this a bottom-up process in which each community selects its priorities? Or is it a top-down arrangement, in which Congress sets the goals and the community has only a limited say?

• The current land management planning process is unclear about which decisions are made at which points in the planning process. No public organization or management system can be effective without clearly articulated goals and an unambiguous decisionmaking process, and in current planning, neither of these conditions obtains.

• The purposes of public participation in federal resource management remain unclear. What is the goal of public participation? How much participation and what quality of participation are necessary for which decisions? In some cases participation at the local level by citizens and interest groups seems to have paralyzed implementation of agreed-upon national or regional policy goals.

• Both natural resources monitoring and program implementation monitoring are currently inadequate. Although immense amounts of data are gathered, useful information about resource conditions and agency performance is often inadequate.

• Funding is not adequately related to management priorities. Historically, sales of commodities have contributed revenue to the general treasury. Although receipts and budgets are not directly linked (except in the case of some trust funds and special accounts), they have offset congressional appropriations to some extent. If the mission priorities will mean fewer commodity receipts, Congress and the agencies will have to address funding priorities.

• Budgets are not linked to the resource management plans and monitoring plans, yet all three are tools in the management process.

• Statutory guidance among federal environmental laws and land management laws often conflicts.

Because the problems that exist are both serious and complex, the problems cannot be resolved through regulatory reform or through the appropriations process. Rather, new legislation is warranted. Our national forests and public lands represent an American legacy, and given their importance, new legislation should reflect bipartisan consensus involving both the legislature and the executive.

Our study of the national forests and public lands leads us to make recommendations in three broad areas: clarifying the purposes of the national forests and public lands, improving the land management planning process, and financing federal land management. Many of the recommendations below are structured to set forth the choices that must be made by citizens, legislators, and professional resource managers.

1. Clarifying the Purposes

In the past 20 years, federal environmental laws, court decisions, executive orders, and regulations have increasingly emphasized the importance of protecting ecological processes on the public lands and national forests. These incremental changes have come without a corresponding change in the basic land management statutes. Congress has the constitutional responsibility to set policy for the national forests and public lands and should act decisively to establish clear priorities for their management. Although the legislative intent and organizational goals must be clear, there is also a need for flexible, local implementation that meets local and regional needs. This was the original management philosophy of the Forest Service and the old Grazing Service (predecessor to BLM). We believe it is still an appropriate goal.

The legislative history of the Creative Act of 1891 reveals that the language incorporated in the law had its origin in an earlier bill that was considered but not passed in 1888. Steen (1997, p. 61) writes that the 1888 bill was accompanied by a committee report that "clearly acknowledged the intent to establish forest reserves to protect water supplies."

Six years later Congress refined the purposes statement in the Organic Administration Act (16 U.S.C. 475), writing,

> No national forest shall be established, except to improve and protect the forest within the boundaries, or for the purpose of securing favorable conditions of water flows, and to furnish a continuous supply of timber for the use and necessities of citizens of the United States.

All those original purposes should be understood in the context of the science and politics of the late 19th century, when water supply, flooding, deforestation, and timber famine had risen to the top of the domestic political agenda. The quoted language has been widely cited to affirm the importance of timber production within the national forests, but the other purposes (forest improvement, forest protection, and water supplies) must be given equal weight. More important, congressional concern for the public good is clear in these statutes and the legislative history. The national forests, and later the public lands conserved through the Taylor Act, were established to provide for public values. That is the principle that must guide any new legislative reform.

Public values. Defining public values is at least as complex as defining ecosystem management, multiple use, or sustained yield. A first step in this process is understanding the inherent limitations and advantages of the public and private sectors in our society. Consider the role of government in providing public values. There are some things that governments do well. A partial list might include building transportation systems, supplying public water, managing public health, conserving environmental resources, and ensuring the national defense. At the same time, there are some things that the private sector provides more efficiently than the public sector. Examples in this category include the provision of food and fiber, telecommunications, financial services, and consumer goods.

A continuing tension in natural resources and environmental policy is establishing and then redefining the appropriate roles of the public and private sectors. Recall that our current public land system and regulatory regime are a legacy of the Progressive Movement, which sought to conserve natural resources through public ownership of federal lands and regulation of private forests because existing markets and property systems had failed to protect those resources.

There is significant concern that biodiversity and other ecosystem services are not fully captured in commercial markets and are often given too little weight in policy decisions (Costanza et al. 1997). Our current understanding of ecology leads us to believe that biodiversity plays an important role in sustaining the ecological system essential for human life. Public concern for ecological sustainability represents a modern successor to the historical concerns for flooding, water supply, deforestation, and timber famine that threatened public values when the national forests and, later, the public lands were established.

Since the 1920s the United States has enjoyed remarkable success in growing forests and sustainably producing timber and fiber on private lands (MacCleery 1992). The "timber famine" so feared in the early 20th century did not occur because a combination of markets and government programs made private forestry possible and profitable.

Given that success, a policy analyst might reasonably ask why the federal government should now be in the business of selling public natural resources except where it facilitates clearly articulated public values. These values include harvesting timber where it protects and improves the forest (forest health), improves water flows (watershed management), or provides a continuous supply of timber in local or regional markets where it is not otherwise available.

If "improving and protecting the forest"—in modern terms, ensuring ecosystem health, including biodiversity—are the primary purposes of public forest management, then timber harvest and all other uses should be evaluated as vegetation management tools to achieve those ends. Meeting ecological objectives and cost effectiveness would become the basis for deciding which tools best meet management prescriptions.

Ecosystem management versus the working forest. Lawmakers and regulators will soon be asked to choose between two competing visions of the national forests and public lands. The first is often labeled ecosystem management (and more recently, ecological sustainability). This vision recognizes the importance of ecological systems and the role of biological diversity in sustaining nutrient and energy cycling. Production of some commodities and other uses may be subordinated to the maintenance of bio-geo-chemical processes.

We label the second alternative the working forest. In this vision, forests are actively managed to meet the economic and social needs of the human community while conserving important ecological processes and functions. Over time, some of these ecosystem processes and functions may be subordinated to meet the economic and social needs of the human community. The working forest is rooted in the original conception of multiple use, but it recognizes that human needs cannot be met without affecting ecosystem integrity.

Readers will quickly note that choosing is really a matter of values. There are questions of science associated with both alternatives, but this is ultimately a political question with scientific implications. Sustainability, as Cohen (1998) writes, "depends, in part…on how many will want parks and how many will want parking lots; on how many will want Jaguars with a capital J and how many will want jaguars with a small j."

Sustainability is not always an either-or choice. Science can best contribute by developing an array of management alternatives that provide as many values as possible and by showing the expected trade-offs among different alternatives. Choosing among the alternatives—and deciding which values gain precedence—is ultimately a political question.

It is important to clarify the implications of choosing a forest vision. New legislation must clarify which of the many legitimate public values are now most important and must balance the economic and ecological consequences of human management of forest and rangeland resources. This task, which lies at the heart of the matter, will entail a political struggle of enormous consequence.

Multiple use. It is appropriate that the national forests and public lands be managed flexibly to meet the changing needs of the nation. For the past 50 years, we have relied on the multiple-use strategy to make the necessary spatial accommodations. The concept of multiple use remains politically popular because it promises many things to all interests, but it does not work at small spatial scales. Multiple use can be employed only at the national or regional level. Congress should clearly articulate in new legislation that the concept of multiple use is not necessarily appropriate on every management unit, but may be better applied in the aggregate across the national forests and public lands.

The national forests and public lands are now managed on an adjacent dominant-use basis, with some areas managed as ecological reserves, some as watersheds, some as recreation areas, and some for timber and fiber production. On a systemwide basis this roughly equates to multiple use. But a locally or regionally articulated dominant-use or key-values approach that relies on area allocation will not, of itself, reduce the conflict until there is some agreement about the purposes, and relative importance, of different values and products.

What shall we sustain? A fundamental problem in forestry is that the doctrine of sustained yield has historically been applied to timber management without adequate regard for the other values that derive from the national forests and public lands (Behan 1992). The modern adaptation of the sustained yield concept is that forests should sustain healthy, resilient ecosystems, not just timber production. The assumption of sustainable forestry is that if ecological processes remain intact, the products of the forests, deserts, and grasslands will remain available for human consumption. If Congress wants to retain sustained yield as a tenet, it must clearly say so and then broaden the definition to include all the legislated public values associated with the national forests and public lands.

Conflicting legislation. A major issue for almost all public agencies is how to take vague and even conflicting laws, translate them into programs, and implement them in an environment of adversarial legalism (O'Leary et al. 1997). In the past two decades the Forest Service and the Bureau of Land Management have begun to reinterpret their missions in light of changing judicial interpretation, public values, and new federal environmental laws. This reinterpretation comes without a corresponding change in the land management statutes. As a result, the tension between the agencies and their legislative oversight committees has increased. In the absence of agreement, the role of the courts has increased.

In many situations, the guiding laws are the Endangered Species Act, the Clean Water Act, or the Clean Air Act—individually or in combination. The manner in which they are coordinated must be clarified. Fragmented authority and different policy goals among the Environmental Protection Agency, the Fish and Wildlife Service, the National Marine Fisheries Service, and the states have often combined to delay or even prevent sound resource management (GAO 1996).

Consistent with sound management theory, the federal land management agencies should be given broad authority and responsibility to meet all environmental requirements. Consultation is appropriate, but other federal and state agencies should not have the responsibility for approving land management activities. If the federal land management agencies do not act in a prudent, responsible fashion, their actions should be subject to legal challenges.

2. Improving the Planning Process

More than 20 years ago, Congress and agency managers made the assumption that applying a locally based, rational, and comprehensive land-use planning process to the national forests and public lands would result in effective natural resources management. Today, we recognize that our current planning process does not resolve fundamental differences of values.

Land-use planning on the national forests and public lands has become so complex that professional advocates now dominate the process. Recent administrations have failed to revise and implement national forest planning regulations in a timely fashion. Given the polarization of the executive and the legislature, we are skeptical that regulatory reform can now succeed.

In 1998 the Clinton administration asked a committee of scientists to review national forest planning regulations. The committee advocated a management paradigm for the national forests based on protecting ecological sustainability; the committee also supported continuing and intensifying citizen participation in the planning process. It is unclear how overlaying this guidance on the already complex regulatory framework will affect natural resources management.

There is consensus that the national forest and public land planning process needs to be improved, but the consensus seems to break down as the specificity of the recommendation increases. An important question to ask about planning relates to its cost effectiveness.

The Forest Service estimated that it had spent more than $250 million on forest plans between 1977 and 1996 (GAO 1996). The plans often took three to 10 years to develop and had a planning horizon of 10 to 15 years. Are the costs justified by the results?

The past 20 years has demonstrated that complex, long-range federal land management planning does not necessarily result in flexible, coherent resource conservation that meets the rapidly changing set of public values. There are many reasons for this failure, and they are well documented in a series of reports from the General Accounting Office, the Congressional Research Service, and the Office of Technology Assessment. Planning and managing for the harmonious conservation of all public values on the national forests and public lands are not currently cost effective and may never be practical, but improvements would meet the following objectives:

• Resource management plans and subsequent monitoring strategies should provide an appropriate range of diverse, resilient aquatic, and terrestrial communities.

• Resource management plans should identify and quantify (to the extent feasible) appropriate goals and outcomes, including vegetation management goals and commodity and amenity outputs.

• The plans should compare and contrast the goals and outcomes with recent performance, highlighting situations where a significant change in direction is proposed.

• Plans should indicate expected financial performance and expected economic and environmental consequences (including economic and social stability, downstream air and water quality, and other environmental effects).

• The goals and outputs (including fiscal expectations and downstream effects) should be set forth in a manner that provides a basis for monitoring, evaluating, and reporting agency performance.

• Any legislation to improve the planning process should be clear in its relationship to existing planning legislation.

Many informed recommendations for change in the planning process have been advanced. MacCleery (1998) offers eight coherent recommendations that address (1) modifying collaborative approaches, (2) changing the role of the interdisciplinary team, (3) shifting the focus of planning alternatives, (4) changing the analysis of the management situation, (5) developing criteria and indicators for sustainable forest management, (6) resolving spatial scale issues, (7) changing timber management, and (8) changing budget procedures.

Citizen participation versus professional discretion. Both citizen participation and professional discretion are important in resource management planning. Under current federal law, the responsible official who must make the difficult management decisions is a professional resource manager. Citizens clearly have a responsibility to make their wishes known, and professional resource managers have a duty to listen carefully to the public.

New legislation—and the regulatory language that implements it—should explicitly acknowledge that both professional resource managers and the public have roles in the planning and management process. The general trend has been to increase the role of public participation in natural resource management, but the current public participation process in NFMA is cumbersome and often ineffective. The national forests and public lands are public resources, not common resources (Hardin 1962), and at some point management decisions must be made and implemented.

What is the goal of public participation? It should ensure that all reasonable ideas are considered. It must gauge the sentiments of the affected publics. It may introduce creative ideas and methods for finding resource management solutions and foster better decisions. Local public participation should not paralyze implementation of national and regional policy goals, which should be shaped through national and regional processes.

Public participation occurs at several levels and in several forms in our system of government. National interest groups compete with each other to shape legislative mandates at the national level. Regional interests and state governments attempt to influence regional guidance. Local interests attempt to shape local decisions. What is unclear in this process is which decisions are negotiable at which spatial scale.

In recent years there have been some successes with representative (rather than the democratic) participation processes. The Catskill Watershed Agreement in New York State (Catskill 1997) and several recent advisory processes convened by state governors (Western Governors Association 1998) provide a model that federal land managers should consider.

Administrative appeals. Solutions to the problem of appeals vary so widely that we offer several alternatives:

1. Eliminate the Forest Service appeals process enacted in the fiscal year 1993 Interior Appropriations Act.

2. Adopt the BLM appeals process for the National Forest System, including the administrative law functions currently in use by the Interior Board of Land Appeals.

3. Increase the requirements for filing an administrative appeal by requiring participation in the decision process related to the specific decision.

4. Revise the National Environmental Policy Act (NEPA) decision process in the following way. First, publish a scoping document that lists alternatives but does not propose a preferred option. Second, propose a resource management plan or management action based on the scoping document and public comments received in the first round. The proposed plan or action is then subject to public comment and review. Third, make a formal decision. The decision would not be subject to administrative appeal but could be challenged in court.

5. Have the president's Council on Environmental Quality administer the appeals process, instead of the agency. This suggestion acknowledges the political nature of the appeals process and would require that the administration clearly articulate its policy goals.

Spatial scales. Once the overall mission of the lands has been identified, the most important questions about land management planning on the national forests and public lands relate to clarifying which issues are decided at which levels of the decisionmaking process. We reiterate: no organization or management system can be effective without clearly articulated goals and an unambiguous decisionmaking process. In the current planning process, neither of these conditions obtains.

Forest planning regulations should identify the analyses and decisions that must be made at each planning level. Forest or area plans might be the appropriate place to analyze and decide wilderness recommendations, output targets, supply-demand relationships, and community impacts. Watershed or landscape plans might be the appropriate place to analyze and decide on silvicultural practices and restoration activities and the mix of habitats necessary for species viability. Activity plans might be the appropriate place to analyze and decide access and management unit boundaries.

Although the number of planning levels should be manageable, our concern is not so much the number of planning levels as it is knowing the who, what, when, and where of plans and decisions. If the process is clear to both citizens and managers, appropriate information can be brought to bear on the questions. This will help participants raise relevant issues at the proper time.

Monitoring. There are at least two issues associated with monitoring on the national forests and public lands. The first is monitoring the condition and trend of the natural resources. Forest or area plans should identify necessary monitoring as well as the type, location, and intensity of measurements needed. Monitoring should be cost effective and should concentrate on important outcomes. The monitoring plan should be part of the decision document.

Resource monitoring gives agency managers an opportunity to involve stakeholders in the public management process. For example, in range trend monitoring, grazing permittees and other interested parties often gather data under the supervision of the resource management staff. Sharing data and learning monitoring techniques can build public support for resource management.

The second type of monitoring focuses on agency performance. The GAO has been particularly critical of Forest Service program monitoring and strategic planning under the Government Performance and Results Act of 1993 (GAO 1997).

Developing and incorporating useful criteria and indicators are essential parts of the monitoring process. The National Association of State Foresters is providing substantial leadership in reviewing and adapting the sustainability criteria and indicators from the Montreal Process. New legislation should carefully evaluate the advantages and disadvantages of adopting a shared set of criteria and indicators that can be adapted for resource and agency performance monitoring.

A separate recommendation, under "Financing Land Management" (below), addresses funding for monitoring programs.

New information. Events that occur after a resource management plan is adopted can significantly alter the subsequent allocation decisions. Changing budgets, appropriations riders, policy decisions at the Council on Environmental Quality or in the secretary of Agriculture or Interior's office sometimes challenge the delicate compromises and understandings of local planning participants. There is also a legitimate concern about how to treat new, scientifically credible information.

Planning regulations should provide a systematic means for addressing new information, including the results of monitoring. The process should include ways to preserve or protect values of concern while the new information is examined for scientific validity and incorporated into analyses and decisions, but without overriding or invalidating the planned targets and budgets. It should also include ways to respond to new ideas — to alter plans and actions expeditiously when valid information is identified, and to test new or unproven ideas.

The authors divided over how much certainty resource management plans should provide to resource users. Several of us were adamant that once plans have allocated resources, new information should not alter the allocations until the plans have been amended. Others suggested that this is an issue of professional discretion—that whether a planning goal should be altered in the face of new information should be left to the discretion of the decisionmaker. We did not reach consensus on this issue.

Experimentation and innovation. One of the most striking and difficult parts of the debate over the national forests and public lands centers on how centralized or dispersed their management should be. Modern organizational theory supports the idea that units should be responsive to the concerns of their stakeholders within the broad outlines of national policy. Simply stating the principle, however, does not resolve the problem. Analysts, employees, and stakeholders know that the combination of statutes, executive orders, administrative regulations, and judicial decisions constrains management flexibility and innovation.

Naturally, shifting the level of policy guidance has strategic advantages and disadvantages for different interests. Nonetheless, new legislation and administrative regulations should stimulate and carefully evaluate innovative, consensus-based approaches to management that arise from broadly represented communities.

Experimentation should be encouraged, but it should be limited to certain conditions. Authority for experiments should be constrained until the agencies have demonstrated that they can monitor and report results and consequences in a manner that satisfies representative stakeholders. When this ability is proven, the agencies may be authorized to test innovative management options that might not comply with current regulations.

Such experiments should (1) identify the spatial, temporal, and financial boundaries of the test; (2) identify the expected results and consequences of the activities, including the lowest acceptable results and the greatest acceptable consequences; (3) identify the monitoring that will occur; (4) identify mitigation and other actions that will occur if the results and consequences exceed acceptable limits; and (5) report, both internally and to the public, on the experiments and the results. Finally, managers should be rewarded for creative innovation. Some failures will result, but managers should not be penalized unless they fail to implement agreed-upon mitigation strategies.

3. Financing Land Management

The consequences of changing management. One of the most apparent effects of changing timber harvest levels on the national forests and public lands has been the change in financing land management. As court decisions and recent administrations have shifted emphasis away from commodity production to protection of biodiversity and watershed restoration, timber receipts have declined. Although the national forests have never been financially self-sufficient, grazing and timber receipts have offset some of the costs of management. If timber harvest will now be pursued in support of other vegetation management objectives rather than for revenue production, the ways in which public land management is financed will also have to change. One can make a convincing argument that the most valuable resource produced on the national forests and public lands of the West is water. If watershed management will be reemphasized on these public lands, Congress must address how to pay for it, or how it may pay for itself. Experimental programs for collecting revenues from recreational users and nontraditional forest products should be expanded.[1]

Management decisions are influenced by appropriations decisions because budgeting reinforces program priorities. If appropriations and agency-articulated management priorities are not consistent, managers and stakeholders receive mixed messages. There is an explicit link between appropriations and system outputs, and management planning that ignores that connection is meaningless.

The effects of the budget. A persistent criticism of resource management plans is that annual appropriations have not always matched the funding assumptions. Forest or area plans should explain how the goals and outcomes would be affected by differing budgets. Annual reporting on agency performance can then compare and contrast the goals and targets of the plan with the requested budgets and actual appropriations.

Funding a monitoring program. Monitoring should be separately and adequately funded. To help assure adequate financing, activity funding and implementation (e.g., for timber sales or watershed projects) could be linked to fulfilling the monitoring promises in the forest or area plans.

Trust funds and special accounts. Use of the trust funds and special accounts should be reviewed and modified. Administrative reform is warranted before legislative changes are considered. The agencies should use care to ensure that projects funded through these accounts meet the legislative intent Congress had when developing the accounts.

• Congress should continue to examine the adequacy of payments in lieu of taxes and other compensation programs to compensate the states and counties fairly and consistently for the tax-exempt status of federal lands.

• The Forest Service's Salvage Sale Fund and Knutson-Vandenberg Fund and the BLM's Forest Ecosystem Health and Recovery Fund are particularly important tools for ensuring that money will be available for rehabilitating damaged forests and regenerating harvested stands in a timely fashion. Reallocating program funds or seeking supplemental appropriations often cannot occur rapidly enough to deal with the damage to soil and water resources that can follow fires and other disturbances.

• Although the trust funds and special accounts are necessary, there is also a need for better accountability. The oversight committees of the legislature and the agencies should pay close attention to this issue.

---

[1]Increases in user fees and permits may prove costly, however. Someone who suffers an accident on federal land and sues the agency bears a lower burden of proof if he or she has paid a fee for use of the land. Legislation that exempts federal land managers from suits unless the plaintiff can prove gross or willful and wanton acts of negligence may be appropriate.

Appendix 1

National Forest and Public Lands Outputs

The National Forest System

The Forest Service manages 191 million acres of the National Forest System under a variety of statutes. Management objectives include sustainable yields of timber, recreation, forage, wildlife, and water. Once based on a "conservation philosophy committed to wise use and balanced consideration of all natural resources," Forest Service management proposals have shifted over the past decade to an "ecological approach" (FS 1986, 1993).

Statistics on timber, recreation, grazing, water resources, and threatened and endangered species are presented in this report. The analysis comprises 11 years of output information—from fiscal years 1986 through 1996. Also included is a brief statistical history of timber harvest volumes from 1911.

Timber. The Forest Service reported an all-time record timber volume harvest of 12.7 billion board feet (bbf) in 1987. Two years later, in 1989, the harvest fell by 0.8 bbf because of injunctions over the northern spotted owl and appeals on individual timber sales. The 1991 decrease of 4.2 bbf, or about 33.3 percent from 1987, to 8.4 bbf in harvested timber reflects Forest Service management actions in response to concerns about the northern spotted owl, the red-cockaded woodpecker, and old-growth forest protection. Increased delays resulting from administrative appeals and litigation contributed to the lower harvests and sales. Harvest levels, offered timber volumes, and sale volumes continued to decline through 1995 to 3.9 bbf, 4.0 bbf, and 2.9 bbf respectively; those figures represent decreases of 69.6 percent, 65.2 percent, and 74.5 percent, respectively, from 1987 figures.

The high levels of timber harvested in 1987 reflect an increase in demand for timber products; the related sales figures represent an increase in the average bid price, up 29 percent from the previous year. The number of sales reached 366,874 in 1985, then began to decrease, with some fluctuation throughout the years, to 215,004 sales in 1994 and 216,272 sales in 1995. The value of timber sold also declined, from a high of $1.3 billion in 1989 to approximately $370 million in 1995. In its 1994 Report of the Forest Service, the agency attributed the lower volumes to "unexpected litigations, appeals and consultation timeframes" associated with newly listed threatened, endangered, and sensitive species. Adding to the reduction is the ongoing public debate over long-term national forest management objectives.

Harvest volumes had grown steadily, from 0.37 bbf in 1911 to 12.3 bbf in 1973. After 1973, timber harvest volumes declined by nearly half, to a low of 6.7 bbf in 1982, then sharply increased in the five years leading up to the record harvest of 12.7 bbf in 1987.

Stabilization of timber offerings and sales may be attributed to the President's Forest Plan for the Northwest in 1994 and the 1995 Emergency Timber Salvage Act, under the 1995 Rescissions Act. The long-term reduction in timber offered for sale results partly from commitments to incorporate ecosystem management principles into the agency's approach to management and to reduce the use of clearcutting as a harvest method (FS 1994).

In 1995, 493 million board feet was offered for sale under the president's plan, plus 1.8 billion board feet of salvaged timber—more than half the total volume offered for sale that year. The Forest Service accomplished 74 percent of the planned harvest in 1994, 94 percent in 1995, and 89 percent in 1996 (Culbert pers. commun.). This progress is also attributed to the president's plan and the salvage act. Reasons for not meeting 100 percent of planned volumes stem from what the Forest Service calls "rework" and ongoing litigation and injunctions, such as the Mexican spotted owl injunction in Arizona and New Mexico.

Recreation. Measured in recreation visitor days (RVD), recreation use on the National Forest System steadily increased for 10 years starting in

1986. The 1986 figure—226.5 million RVDs—represented 43 percent of total recreation on federal lands. As of 1995, there were 345.1 million RDVs on Forest Service lands, a 52.3 percent increase. In 1996 the Forest Service reported 341.1 million RVDs—a 1.4 percent decrease from 1995. Despite this decrease, there was an increase in total visits on National Forest System lands, from 691.1 million visits in 1992 to 859.3 million visits in 1996—a 24.3 percent increase—as well as an increase from 1995 (829.7 million visits) to 1996. These figures include consumptive as well as nonconsumptive activities, mechanized and water travel, and other recreation activities. Mechanized activities increased the most, in RVDs, on Forest Service lands.

Hunting and fishing uses continue to increase on the national forests, but their percentage of overall recreation activity has decreased. Consumptive activities rose from 30.5 million RVDs in 1986 to 36.7 million RVDs in 1995. Hunting and fishing accounted for 10.6 percent of total recreation use in 1995. In 1986 hunting and fishing represented 13.4 percent of recreation activities. Nonconsumptive fish and wildlife use also continues to rise. The figure for 1991 is 2.2 million RVDs compared with 3.2 million in 1995—a 42.8 percent increase over five years and an increase in recreation shares by 0.12 percent. By 1996, the percent of nonconsumptive activities accounted for only 0.38 percent of total recreation visitor days.

For a few years before 1986, recreation use declined. The Forest Service, in its 1986 annual report, mentions site deterioration and refinements in counting RVDs as possible causes. That same year, recreation use away from facilities accounted for approximately 66 percent of total use. The subsequent increase in use does not involve improvements in facilities.

Those data may contain some inaccuracies. Fee sites and activities requiring a permit provide more reliable counts of recreation, but only for those particular situations, not for total recreational use. Visits to the national forests are likely increasing, however, and as more fees and permits are collected to maintain the forests despite the increased use, better measures of recreation use may become available.

Livestock grazing. In 1986 the number of animal unit months (AUM) permitted to graze was 10.1 million, spread over 102 million acres in 36 states. Actual grazing use was 8.6 million AUMs on 53 percent of national forest land. The reason for this difference stems from the economic conditions affecting the livestock industry (FS 1986). The amount of livestock permitted to graze declined throughout the 11 years to 9.3 million AUMs in both 1994 and 1995, and 9.2 million AUMs in 1996. Decreases reflect implementation of Forest Service plans to balance resource values and outputs (FS 1993).

The Forest Service does not have a definition of rangeland health or a methodology to assess rangeland condition at this time, so no true indicator of rangeland condition exists (Holtrop pers. commun.). Permits to graze are distributed at 10-year intervals, but the number of AUMs authorized to graze is derived on an annual basis under the 10-year plan. Fluctuations in these numbers are mainly due to market conditions and resource conditions, such as drought and fire history.

Threatened and endangered species. Plants and animals listed as threatened and endangered on Forest Service lands rose from 141 species in 1986 to 283 species in 1995. Nationally, the number of species has increased 69.9 percent within the last seven years. Listed plant species on Forest Service lands rose from 48 species in 1989 to 110 species in 1995. Figures for listed animal species follow.

Threatened and Endangered Animal Species

	1989	1995
Mammals	21	27
Insects	4	9
Fish	39	52
Birds	24	31
Snails, mussels, crustaceans	26	40
Reptiles, amphibians	9	14

Forest Service lands housed 29 percent of listed species in the United States in 1995 and 1996. This percentage has remained relatively constant throughout the period.

Water resources. The Forest Service has recently begun to look at the condition of watersheds. Since 1987 the number of recorded watersheds on Forest Service lands has been changing. From 1987 to 1989 the number of watersheds dropped by 32, from 3,160 to 3,128 (LaFayette pers. commun.).

Watershed condition classes, as defined by the Forest Service, are "a relative description of the health of a watershed as measured against management objectives in terms of the factors that affect favorable conditions of water flow and soil capability." The classifications are useful as a general guide only; there exists no one method to measure watershed quality or function in an accurate and acceptable manner.

Condition of Watersheds

	1987		1989	
Class I	900	28.5%	1,194	38.2%
Class II	1,630	51.6	1,418	45.3
Class III	630	19.9	516	16.5

Bureau of Land Management

The Bureau of Land Management (BLM) manages approximately 264 million acres of federal land, or about 12.5 percent of the land in the United States. In 1990 management of public lands stemmed from principles of multiple use and sustained yield. Since then, demands have changed, and so has the BLM's land-management scheme, to a landscape or "big picture" approach (BLM 1996).

The 264 million acres managed by BLM in fiscal year 1996 include 2.6 million acres of Oregon and California (O&C) revested lands in western Oregon. In 1990 the BLM managed 272 million acres, or 41 percent of federally owned lands, so the 1996 figure represents a decline in land area. Approximately one third of BLM's land is in Alaska, and that proportion has remained constant over the past 10 years, as has the O&C figure.

Following are BLM statistics for timber, recreation, grazing, and threatened and endangered species for 1987 to 1996, plus water resource quality from 1995 and 1996. Timber statistics include current 1997 harvest information and a brief statistical history of timber volume sales as well.

Timber. Within the past 11 years, harvest levels reached a high in 1988 at approximately 1.74 bbf (Costello pers. commun.); O&C lands contributed nearly 1.68 bbf to that level, or 96.5 percent. Western Oregon lands consistently provide the majority of timber harvested and sold. Timber harvest volumes totaled 0.16 bbf in 1997, down 87.4 percent from 1988. The timber volume harvested from O&C lands decreased 93.2 percent from 1988 to 1997. The number of acres harvested on BLM lands in 1988 totaled 51,443, compared with 13,729 acres of harvested land in 1997—a decrease of 37,714 acres, or about 73.3 percent in the past 10 years. The numbers fluctuated within those years from a high of 61,286 acres in 1992 to a low of 10,682 acres in 1995.

Generally, since the 1960s to the mid-1980s, timber sales have remained slightly above 1 bbf. Sales grew to 1.7 bbf in 1963, then declined to 1 bbf in 1985. An increase of 0.51 bbf took place between 1985 and

1986, bringing timber volume sold to 1.5 bbf—the highest volume reached over the past 20 years.

Injunctions dealing with the northern spotted owl "virtually halted Western Oregon's entire timber sale program" (BLM 1992, 1993). The decrease in harvested volume and sales from the early 1990s results from environmental concerns about protecting northern spotted owl and salmon habitat, old-growth forest preservation, litigation, and BLM's move toward new management plans. BLM met and exceeded its targets to offer 127 million board feet for 1995 under the Northwest Forest Plan; its 1996 target was to offer 180 million board feet, and for 1997, 211 million board feet (Hayes 1996).

Recreation. Recreation use on BLM lands increased throughout the years by 75.9 percent, from 41.3 million RVDs in 1987 to 72.8 RVDs in 1996. Hunting and fishing RVDs also increased by 61.9 percent for the same period. Throughout the years, the recreation activities reported by the BLM have changed, so a comparison between activities is not included here. US Fish and Wildlife Service reports (the 1991 and 1985 national survey of fishing, hunting, and wildlife-associated recreation) served as a basis for hunting data: 8.4 million hunter days for 1987–92 and 37.0 million hunter days for 1993–96, a 338.7 percent increase from one five-year period to the next.

Those data may include inaccuracies in measuring wildlife-related recreation on BLM lands. The differences in participant numbers may be attributed to incomplete data, to new methods of counting RVDs through the years, or to the lack of tools to keep track of activities on public lands.

Livestock grazing. This report combines figures for authorized use under Section 3 and Section 15 of FLPMA; it also combines permits and leases in force under the two sections of the law.

Both authorized use and permits and leases in force have been declining. In 1987 authorized use was 11.2 million AUMs, and the figure for permits and leases in force was 14.4 million AUMs. Authorized use declined 12.9 percent to 9.7 million AUMs over the period, and permits and leases decreased 9.3 percent to 13.1 million AUMs. Changes in the condition of rangelands, herd size, sales, and deaths contribute to the number of authorized users from year to year.

Threatened and endangered species. The number of threatened and endangered plant and animal species rose from 140 listed species in 1987 to 228 listed species in 1996 (Fielder and Berg, pers. commun.). Information is not available for the total number of listed species for the years 1990, 1991, 1993, and 1994. Animal species include mammals, birds, fish, amphibians, reptiles and invertebrates. The individual states' listed species have been tracked for the past 10 years. Of the 12 represented states for 1996, eastern states (which count as one state but include all states bordering on or east of the Mississippi) contain the largest number of listed plant (131) and animal species (184).

Water resources. The Bureau of Land Management began including conditions of riparian-wetland areas in public land statistics in 1995. These areas, divided into riparian miles and wetland acres, are classified into four conditions: proper functioning condition, functional at risk, nonfunctional, and unknown. The total number of riparian miles in 1995 and 1996 is 180,613 miles and 180,595 miles, respectively—a decrease of 18 miles. The total area of wetlands is approximately 16.1 million acres; in 1996 BLM reported an increase of 21,982 acres from 1995.

In 1996, 79.5 percent of riparian miles were in proper functioning condition, compared with 78.9 percent in 1995. The number of miles classified as functional at risk and nonfunctional also increased slightly, from 7.3 percent and 3.1 percent in 1995, respectively, to 7.9 percent and 3.2 percent, respectively, in 1996. The number of riparian miles whose condition was unknown decreased from 10.9 percent in 1995 to 9.4 percent in 1996.

A large percentage, 20.5 percent, of wetland acres was classified as unknown for both years. Wetland acres in proper functioning condition also remained about the same, at 78.5 percent for 1995 and 78.6 percent for 1996. The percentage of functional at risk and nonfunctional wetland acres remained small, less than 1 percent each for both years.

How much water BLM lands produce—that is, the water that flows from the watershed across public land to a boundary, not including yield from groundwater sources—is estimated at 10 million acre feet annually (Janes, pers. commun.). This is an average and includes the 12 western and Rocky Mountain states, excluding the Dakotas and Great Plains. This best estimate is rough but nevertheless provides an idea of the water flow on BLM lands.

Appendix 2

Major Laws Pertaining to the National Forests and Public Lands

General Mining Law of 1872, 17 Stat. 91

Creative Act of 1891, 26 Stat. 1103

Organic Administration Act of 1897, 30 Stat. 11

Transfer Act of 1905, 33 Stat. 628

Preservation of American Antiquities Act of 1906, 34 Stat. 225

Twenty-Five Percent Fund Act of 1908, 35 Stat. 251

Weeks Law, Act of 1911, 36 Stat. 961

Timber Export, Act of 1917, 39 Stat. 1134

Mineral Leasing Act of 1920, 41 Stat. 437

Fish and Wildlife Coordination Act of 1934, 48 Stat. 401

Taylor Grazing Act of 1934, 48 Stat. 1269

Oregon and California Revested Lands Sustained Yield Management Act of 1937 (O&C), 50 Stat. 874

Sustained Yield Forest Management Act of 1944, 58 Stat. 132

Watershed Protection and Flood Control Act of 1954, 68 Stat. 666

Clean Air Act of 1955, 69 Stat. 322, as amended

Mining Claims Rights Restoration Act of 1955, 69 Stat. 681

Multiple Use and Sustained Yield Act of 1960 (MUSY), 74 Stat. 215

Sikes Act of 1960 (Fish and Wildlife Conservation Act), 74 Stat. 1052

Wilderness Act of 1964, 78 Stat. 890

Multiple Use and Land Classification Act of 1964, 78 Stat. 986

National Forest Roads and Trails Act of 1964, 78 Stat. 1089

Water Resources Planning Act of 1965, 79 Stat. 244

Historic Preservation Act of 1966, 80 Stat. 915

Wild and Scenic Rivers Act of 1968, 82 Stat. 906

National Trails System Act of 1968, 82 Stat. 919

National Environmental Policy Act of 1969 (NEPA), 83 Stat. 852

Environmental Quality Improvement Act of 1970, 84 Stat. 114

Mining and Minerals Policy Act of 1970, 84 Stat. 1876

Wild Horses and Burros Protection Act of 1971, 85 Stat. 649

Clean Water Amendments of 1972, 86 Stat. 816

Federal Insecticide, Rodenticide, and Fungicide Act of 1972, 86 Stat. 973

Endangered Species Act of 1973, 87 Stat. 884

Preservation of Historical and Archaeological Data Act of 1974, 88 Stat. 174

Forest and Rangeland Renewable Resources Planning Act of 1974 (RPA), 86 Stat. 476

Freedom of Information Act of 1974, 88 Stat. 1561

Eastern Wilderness Act of 1975, 88 Stat. 2096

Toxic Substances Control Act of 1976, 90 Stat. 2003

Payments in Lieu of Taxes Act of 1976 (PILT), 90 Stat. 2662

Federal Land Policy and Management Act of 1976 (FLPMA), 90 Stat. 2743

National Forest Management Act of 1976 (NFMA), 90 Stat 2949

Clean Air Act Amendments of 1977, 91 Stat. 685

Safe Drinking Water Amendments of 1977, 91 Stat. 1393

Soil and Water Resources Conservation Act of 1977, 91 Stat. 1407

American Indian Religious Freedom Act of 1978, 92 Stat. 469

Energy Security Act of 1980, 94 Stat. 611, Title II, Section 262

National Aquaculture Act of 1980, 94 Stat. 1198

Fish and Wildlife Conservation Act of 1980, 94 Stat. 1322

Reforestation Tax Incentives and Trust Fund of 1980, 94 Stat. 1983

Alaska National Interest Land Conservation Act of 1980, 94 Stat. 2457

RPA Statement of Policy of 1980, 94 Stat. 2957

National Historic Preservation Act Amendments of 1980, 94 Stat. 2987

Donation of Real Property to United States Act of 1980, 94 Stat. 3207

Wood Residue Utilization Act of 1980, 94 Stat. 3257

Salmon and Steelhead Resource Conservation Act of 1980, 94 Stat. 3275

Lacey Act Amendments of 1981, 95 Stat. 1073

Agriculture and Food Act of 1981, 95 Stat. 1213

Money and Finance Act of 1982, 96 Stat. 1005

Small Tracts Act of 1983, 97 Stat. 2535

Federal Timber Contract Payment Modification Act of 1984, 98 Stat. 2213

Food Security Act of 1985 (1985 Farm Bill), 99 Stat. 1354

National Forest Ski Area Permit Act of 1986, 100 Stat. 3000

National Forest Drug Control Act of 1986, 100 Stat. 3207-191

Federal Land Exchange Facilitation Act of 1988, 102 Stat. 1986

Rails to Trails (National Trails System Improvement Act of 1988), 102 Stat. 2281

Forest Ecosystems and Atmospheric Pollution Research Act, 1988, 102 Stat. 2601

Federal Energy Management Improvement Act of 1988, 102 Stat. 3185

Anti-Drug Abuse Amendments Act of 1988, 102 Stat. 4362

Federal Cave Resources Protection Act of 1988, 102 Stat. 4546

North American Wetlands Conservation Act of 1989, 103 Stat. 1968

Americans with Disabilities Act of 1990, 104 Stat. 328

Forest Resource Conservation and Shortage Relief Act of 1990, 104 Stat. 714

International Forestry Cooperation Act of 1990, 104 Stat. 2070

Native American Graves Protection and Repatriation Act of 1990, 104 Stat. 3048

Forest Stewardship Act of 1990 (1990 Farm Bill), 104 Stat. 3521

National Environmental Education Act of 1990, 104 Stat. 3552

National Forest-Dependent Rural Communities Economics Diversification Act of 1990, 104 Stat. 3632

Global Climate Change Prevention Act of 1990, 104 Stat. 4058

ISTEA (Intermodal Surface Transportation Efficiency Act) of 1991, 105 Stat. 1930

Scenic Byways Act of 1991, 105 Stat. 1996

Symms National Recreation Trails Act of 1991, 105 Stat. 2064

Pacific Yew Act of 1992, 106 Stat. 859

Salvage Rider of 1995, 109 Stat. 240

Forest Service Permanently Appropriated Trust Funds and Special Accounts.

Payments to States, National Forest Fund: $260.4 million (FY 1996).
Source: 25% of receipts (NFF receipts, plus deposits to the Knutson-Vandenberg Fund and to the Salvage Sale Fund, and road credits).
Use: To compensate counties for tax-exempt lands; for use on roads and schools in the counties where the forests are located.

Timber Salvage Sales: $181.2 miliion (FY 1996).
Source: Receipts from designated salvage sales.
Use: To prepare and administer salvage sales, including necessary road construction.

Knutson-Vandenberg Fund: $153.4 million (FY 1996).
Source: Deposits from timber purchasers, and interest on the balance in the account.
Use: To fund reforestation, timber stand improvements, and other resource mitigation and enhancement in timber sale areas.

Other Cooperative Work: $42.8 million (FY 1996).
Source: Deposits from cooperators, plus interest.
Use: To fund resource protection and improvement, including the construction and maintenance of roads, trails, and other facilities and for scaling services, fire protection, etc.

National Forest Roads and Trails: $36.0 million (FY 1996).
Source: 10% of NFF receipts.
Use: To fund road construction (since FY 1982, transferred to Treasury to offset appropriations for road construction).

Reforestation Trust Fund: $30.4 million (FY 1996).
Source: Tariffs on imports of solid wood products, up to $30 million annually, plus interest.
Use: To fund efforts to eliminate the backlog of reforestation and timber stand improvement needs.

Brush Disposal: $17.8 million (FY 1996).
Source: Deposits from timber purchasers.
Use: To dispose of brush and other debris from cutting operations on timber sale areas.

Operation and Maintenance of Quarters: $6.5 million (FY 1996).
Source: Payroll deductions from FS employees.
Use: To operate and maintain quarters.

Timber Roads, Purchaser Elect: $5.9 million (FY 1996).
Source: Receipts from timber sales where qualified purchasers elect to have FS build roads.
Use: To have FS build roads on sales where small businesses request.

Payments to Counties, National Grasslands: $5.1 million (FY 1996).
Source: 25% of National Grassland receipts.
Use: To compensate counties for tax-exempt lands; for use on roads and schools in the counties where the grasslands are located.

Restoration of Lands and Improvements: $4.9 million (FY 1996).
Source: Bonds or forfeitures by contractors who fail to meet performance requirements.
Use: To complete work necessary due to failure of contractor.

Recreation Fee Collection Costs: $1.5 million (FY 1996).
Source: Up to 15% of recreation fees.
Use: To fund efforts to collect recreation admission and user fees.

Payments to Minnesota: $1.3 million (FY 1996).
Source: Any unappropriated funds in the NFF; at 0.75% of appraised value of specified land.
Use: To compensate counties for tax-exempt lands in the Boundary Waters Canoe Area.

Smokey Bear and Woodsy Owl: <$0.1 million (FY 1996).
Source: Fees for the use of Smokey Bear and Woodsy Owl characters by private enterprises.
Use: To promote forest fire prevention and to promote environmental conservation.

Bureau of Land Management Permanently Appropriated Trust Funds and Special Accounts.

Payments to Counties, O&C and CBWR lands: $73.6 million (FY 1996).
Source: 50% of net revenues.
Use: To compensate counties for tax-exempt lands; for use on roads, schools, and other facilities in the counties where the lands are located.

Forest Ecosystem Health and Recovery Fund: $7.0 million (FY 1996).
Source: Federal share of receipts from salvage timber sales.
Use: To prepare, administer, and reforest salvage sales.

Land and Resource Management Trust Fund—CA Off-Highway: $3.5 million (FY 1996).
Source: State of California off-highway vehicles ("green sticker") licenses.
Use: For resource development, protection, management, and improvement.

Land and Resource Management Trust Fund—FLPMA: $3.2 million (FY 1996).
Source: Contributions and donations.
Use: For resource development, protection, management, and improvement.

Expenses, Road Maintenance: $2.0 million (FY 1996).
Source: Deposits from commercial users.
Use: For road maintenance.

Payments to States, Grazing within Grazing Districts: $1.5 million (FY 1996).
Source: 12.5% of grazing fees.
Use: To compensate counties for tax-exempt federal lands.

Payments to States: $1.0 million (FY 1996).
Source: 4% of gross (5% of net) proceeds from sale of lands and resources.
Use: To compensate counties for tax-exempt lands; for use for education or public roads and improvements.

Payments to States, Grazing outside of Grazing Districts: $1.0 million (FY 1996).
Source: 50% of grazing fees.
Use: To compensate counties for tax-exempt federal lands.

Permanent Miscellaneous Trust Funds—Taylor Grazing Act: $0.8 million (FY 1996).
Source: Contributions.
Use: For rangeland improvement.

Payments to States, Mineral Leasing Act: $0.7 million (FY 1996).
Source: 50% of lease revenues (except for 90% in Alaska).
Use: To compensate counties for tax-exempt federal land.

Permanent Miscellaneous Trust Funds—Public Survey: $0.5 million (FY 1996).
Source: Contributions.
Use: For cadastral surveys.

Payments to Counties—National Grasslands: $0.4 million (FY 1996).
Source: 25% of National Grassland Revenues.
Use: To compensate counties for tax-exempt lands; for use on roads and schools in the counties where the grasslands are located.

Recreation Fee Collection Costs: $0.3 million (FY 1996).
Source: Up to 15% of recreation fees.
Use: To fund efforts to collect recreation admission and user fees.

Land and Resource Management Trust Fund—Sikes Act: $0.3 million (FY 1996).
Source: Contributions from state fish and wildlife agencies under the Sikes Act.
Use: To fund the conservation, restoration, management, and improvement of wildlife and wildlife habitat.

Operation and Maintenance of Quarters: $0.3 million (FY 1996).
Source: Payroll deductions from BLM employees.
Use: To operate and maintain quarters.

Payments to Nevada, Land Sales in Clark County: $0.1 million (FY 1996).
Source: 15% of revenues (10% to the county and 5% to the state).
Use: To compensate the county for tax-exempt federal land.

Payments to Oklahoma: <$0.1 million (FY 1996).
Source: 37.5% of Red River oil and gas royalties on certain tribal lands.
Use: To compensate counties for tax-exempt lands; for use on roads.

Permanent Miscellaneous Trust Funds—Trustee Funds, Alaska Townsites: <$0.1 million (FY 1996).
Source: Contributions.
Use: For sale of town lots to non-Native Alaskans.

Appeals to the Forest Service.

Fiscal year	New appeals	Fiscal year	New appeals
1983	584	1990	1,991
1984	439	1991	1,386
1985	581	1992	1,659
1986	1,081	1993	2,902
1987	874	1994	1,802
1988	1,609	1995	900
1989	1,291	1996	1,054

Appeals to the Interior Board of Land Appeals.

Fiscal year	New IBLA appeals
1992	614
1993	689
1994	774
1995	1,088
1996	1,161

Criteria for Improving the Efficiency and Effectiveness of the Decisionmaking Process for Federal Forest Management.

1. Identifying Goals and Objectives

Purpose. Why a decision is needed.

Values and concerns. The values and concerns of those interested in and affected by the decision.

2. Developing Alternatives

Baseline inventories. Identification of the biophysical constraints limiting the feasible choices.

Open-ended process. A broad, inclusive array of options, from any source.

3. Analyzing Alternatives

Thoroughness. The best estimate, or range of estimates, of the expected consequences of the alternatives on the values and concerns.

Openness. Including the public, both for a thorough review of the analyses and to help the public understand the limitations and trade-offs.

Appropriateness. Time and money for analyses to provide information of sufficient, but not excessive, spatial and temporal details without imposing unnecessary delays.

4. Deciding and Implementing

Timeliness. Deadlines for decisions.

Decentralization. Decisions made by the individual who is most responsible for the environmental and economic consequences of the decision.

Transparency. The who-what-when-where-why-and-how of the decision to inform those who must implement the decision, those affected by or interested in the decision, and those who might be asked to review, explain, or defend the decision.

Tracking. The expected benefits and costs and standards for when differences between the expectations and the results become unacceptable, including the monitoring and the likely responses when unacceptable differences are found.

5. Monitoring the Results

Timeliness. Identifying significant changes before the impacts are catastrophic, but without interfering with implementation.

Meaningfulness. Performance measures that evaluate achieving all the goals and objectives (the purposes and the values and concerns).

Cost-effectiveness. Comparing the actual effects with the expectations for the important values and concerns, in sufficient detail.

Literature Cited

Chapter 1. A Tradition of Discord

CLAWSON, M. 1983. *The federal lands revisited.* Washington, DC: Resources for the Future.

CRONON, W. 1983. *Changes in the land: Indians, colonists and the ecology of New England.* New York: Hill and Wang.

DANA, S.T. 1956. *Forest and rangeland policy.* New York: McGraw-Hill.

OLIVER, C., D. ADAMS, T. BONNICKSEN, J. BOWYER, F. CUBBAGE, N. SAMPSON, S. SCHARBAUM, R. WHALEY, and H. WIANT. 1997. Report on forest health of the United States by the Forest Health Science Panel. Center for International Trade in Forest Products. Seattle: University of Washington.

RICHARDSON, E. 1980. *BLM's billion-dollar checkerboard: Managing the O&C lands.* Santa Cruz: Forest History Society.

ROBBINS, W.G. 1997. The social context of forestry: The Pacific Northwest in the 20th century. In *American forests: Nature, culture, and politics,* ed. C. Miller. Lawrence: University of Kansas Press.

STEEN, H.K. 1976. *The US Forest Service: A history.* Seattle: University of Washington Press.

———. 1997. The beginning of the National Forest System. In *American forests: Nature, culture, and politics,* ed. C. Miller. Lawrence: University of Kansas Press.

Chapter 2. Policy Issues

BALDWIN, P. 1997. Federal land management: Appeals and litigation. Overview prepared for a workshop held by the Senate Committee on Energy and Natural Resources. 97-274A. Washington, DC: Congressional Research Service, Library of Congress.

BEHAN, R.W. 1975. Forestry and the end of innocence. *American Forests* 18:16-19; 38-49.

———. 1978. An outsider's view of the National Forest Management Act. *Western Wildlands* Winter:24-34.

———. 1981. RPA/NFMA—Time to punt. *Journal of Forestry* 79(12):97-100.

CORTNER, H.J., and M.A. SHANNON. 1993. Embedding public participation in its political context. *Journal of Forestry* 91(5):14-16.

DANA, S.T. 1956. *Forest and Range Policy.* New York: McGraw-Hill.

DE STEIGUER, J.E. 1994. Can forestry provide the greatest good of the greatest number? *Journal of Forestry* 92(9):22-25.

ELLIOTT, C. 1996. Certification as a policy instrument. In *Certification of forest products: Issues and perspectives,* ed. V. Viana. Washington, DC: Island Press.

FISHER, J. 1997. Feuding families fire at Forest Service. *Lewiston Morning Tribune.* May 28. Lewiston, ID.

FLOYD, D.W. 1993. Managing rangeland resources conflicts. *Rangelands* 15(1):27-30.

GENERAL ACCOUNTING OFFICE (GAO) 1996. Forest Service issues related to management national forests for multiple uses. GAO/TRCED 96-111. Washington, DC.

———. 1997a. Forest Service decision-making: A framework for improving performance. GAO/RCED-97-71. Washington, DC.

———. 1997b. The Results Act: Observations on the Forest Service's May 1997 draft plan. GAO/RCED-97-223. Washington, DC.

GERMAIN, R.H., and D.W. FLOYD. 1996. The Forest Service public participation process: From the "fishbowl" to the "beaten dog syndrome." Poster presented at the Society of American Foresters National Convention. Albuquerque, NM.

GOERGEN, M.T., D.W. FLOYD, and P.G. ASHTON. 1997. An old model for building consensus and a new role for foresters. *Journal of Forestry* 95(1):8–12.

GORTE, R.W., and B.A. CODY. 1995. The Forest Service and Bureau of Land Management: History and analysis of merger proposals. Congressional Research Service report to Congress 95-117.

GREGG, R.F. 1992. Summary. In *Multiple use and sustained yield: Changing philosophies for federal land management.* Congressional Research Service and Committee on Interior and Insular Affairs, USHR 102nd Congress, 2nd Session. Committee Print No. 11. Washington, DC.

HAGENSTEIN, P.R. 1992. Some history of multiple use/sustained yield concepts. In *Multiple use and sustained yield: Changing philosophies for federal land management.* Congressional Research Service and Committee on Interior and Insular Affairs, USHR 102nd Congress, 2nd Session. Committee Print No. 11. Washington, DC.

HILL, L.W. 1997. Testimony on Forest Service appeals. Workshop on federal land planning: Appeals and litigation. US Senate Committee on Energy and Natural Resources, Subcommittee on Forests and Public Land Management. Washington, DC: Anderson Reporting Co.

HIRT, P.W. 1994. *A conspiracy of optimism: Management of the national forests since World War Two.* Lincoln: University of Nebraska Press.

KAUFMAN, H. 1960. *The forest ranger: A study in administrative behavior.* Baltimore: Johns Hopkins University Press.

LIGGETT, C., C. HICKMAN, R. PRAUSA, and N. REYNA. 1995. *Timber program issues: A technical examination of policy options.* 2nd ed. Washington, DC: USDA Forest Service.

MOHAI, P. 1995. Symposium on change in the United States Department of Agriculture Forest Service and its consequences for national forest policy. *Policy Studies Journal* 23(2):247–351.

MURKOWSKI, F., L. CRAIG, D. YOUNG, and H. CHENOWETH. 1998. Joint letter from Senate Energy and Natural Resources Committee and House Resources Committee to Forest Service Chief Mike Dombeck, February 20.

OFFICE OF TECHNOLOGY ASSESSMENT (OTA). 1992. Forest Service Planning: Accommodating Uses, Producing Outputs and Sustaining Ecosystems. OTA-F-505. Washington, DC: US Congress.

O'TOOLE, R. 1988. Reforming the Forest Service. Washington, DC: Island Press.

RANDALL, A. 1987. *Resource economics: An economic approach to natural resource and environmental policy.* 2nd ed. New York: John Wiley & Sons.

SOCIETY OF AMERICAN FORESTERS (SAF). 1989. Community stability. Report of the Society of American Foresters national task force on community stability. Bethesda, MD.

———. 1993. Task force report on sustaining long-term forest health and productivity. Bethesda, MD.

———. 1995. Forest management certification. Report of the Society of American Foresters national task force on forest management certification. Bethesda, MD.

———. 1997. Briefings on forest issues. Bethesda, MD.

TUCHMAN, E.T., K.P. CONNAUGHTON, L.E. FREEDMAN, and C.B. MORIWAKI. 1996. The Northwest forest plan. A report to the president and Congress. Washington, DC: US Department of Agriculture, Office of Forestry and Economic Assistance.

US DEPARTMENT OF AGRICULTURE (USDA-FS). 1997. Report of the Forest Service, fiscal year 1996. Washington, DC.

US DEPARTMENT OF INTERIOR (USDI-BLM). 1996. Bureau of Land Management public land statistics. Available at http://www.blm.gov/nhp/landfacts/pls96.html.

US DEPARTMENT OF INTERIOR (USDI-MMS). 1997. Minerals Management Service royalty management program. Unpublished data. Report ID: ADH239RC. Denver.

Chapter 3. Evaluating Federal Forest Policy and Decisionmaking

ANDERSON, J.E. 1984. *Public policy-making.* New York: CBS College Publishing.

BENTLEY, W.R. 1995. Knowing ourselves: Changing definitions of the forestry profession. *Journal of Forestry* 93(1):12–15.

CLAWSON, M. 1975. *Forests for whom and for what?* Baltimore: Johns Hopkins University Press.

DRUCKER, P. 1974. *Management: Tasks, responsibilities, practices.* New York: Harper and Row.

FAYOL, H. 1949. *General and industrial management* (1925). New York: Pittman.

JONES, C.O. 1984. *An introduction to the study of public policy.* 3rd ed. Pacific Grove, CA: Brooks/Cole Publishing.

OFFICE OF TECHNOLOGY ASSESSMENT (OTA). 1992. Forest Service planning: Accommodating uses, producing outputs, and sustaining ecosystems. OTA-F-505. Washington, DC.

OLIVER, C., D. ADAMS, T. BONNICKSEN, J. BOWYER, F. CUBBAGE, N. SAMPSON, S. SCHARBAUM, J. SEBELIUS, R. WHALEY, and H. WIANT. 1997. Summary report on forest health of the United States. Center for International Trade in Forest Products. Seattle: University of Washington.

Chapter 4. Recommendations

BEHAN, R.W. 1992. The irony of the multiple use/sustained yield concept: Nothing is so powerful as an idea whose time has passed. In *Multiple use and sustained yield: Changing philosophies for federal land management.* Committee Print No. 11. Washington, DC: US House of Representatives, Committee on Interior and Insular Affairs.

CATSKILL CENTER FOR CONSERVATION AND DEVELOPMENT, INC. 1997. Summary guide to the terms of the watershed agreement. Arkville, NY.

COHEN, J. 1998. How many people can the earth support? *New York Review of Books* XLV(15):29–31.

COSTANZA, R., et al. 1997. The value of the world's ecosystem services and natural capital. *Nature* 387:253–60.

DANA, S.T. 1956. *Forest and range policy.* New York: McGraw-Hill.

GENERAL ACCOUNTING OFFICE (GAO). 1996. Forest Service issues relating to its decisionmaking process. GAO/TRCED-96-66. Washington, DC.

———. 1997. The results act: Observations on the Forest Service's May 1997 draft plan. GAO/TRCED-97-223. Washington, DC.

HARDIN, G. 1968. The tragedy of the commons. *Science* 162:1,243–248.

MACCLEERY, D. 1992. *American forests: A history of resiliency and recovery.* Durham, NC: Forest History Society.

———. 1998. National forest mission shift: How to respond to changing public preferences as to how national forest lands should be managed, while maintaining healthy, diverse and productive ecosystems and the economically viable local communities? Unpublished memo.

O'LEARY, R., et al. 1997. *Environmental management: Principles, practices and priorities for public and nonprofit managers.* San Francisco: Jossey Bass.

STEEN, H.K. 1997. The beginning of the National Forest System. In *American forests: Nature, culture and politics,* ed. C. Miller. Lawrence: University of Kansas Press.

WESTERN GOVERNORS ASSOCIATION. 1998. Principles for environmental management in the West. Policy resolution 98-001. Available at http://www.westgov.org/wga/policy/98001.htm.

Appendix 1. National Forest and Public Lands Outputs

BUREAU OF LAND MANAGEMENT (BLM). 1994. Custom report for fiscal year 1994, BLM's timber sale activity consolidated from the pre-1995 TSIS archives.

———. 1995a. Bureauwide timber harvest activity, summary state totals for fiscal year. Bureauwide summary reports for public land statistics. Report PLS-T. Update edition: 9510.14.

———. 1995b. Bureauwide timber sales summary grand totals: Bureauwide summary reports for public land statistics. Report PLS-C. Update edition: 9510.14.

———. 1996a. Bureauwide timber harvest activity, summary state totals for fiscal year. Bureauwide summary reports for public land statistics. Report PLS-T. Update edition: 199610.12.

———. 1996b. Bureauwide timber sales, summary grand totals: Bureauwide summary reports for public land statistics. Report title: PLS-C. Update edition: 199610.12.

———. 1997a. Bureauwide timber harvest activity, summary state totals for fiscal year. Bureauwide summary reports for public land statistics. Report PLS-T. Update edition: 199708.16.

———. 1997b. Bureauwide timber sales, summary grand totals: Bureauwide summary reports for public land statistics. Report PLS-C. Update edition: 199708.16.

———. State office timber harvest report, fiscal year summaries [1986–94]. Report: Harvest. Update Edition: 9507.10.

———. Oregon state office, eastside timber harvest report, fiscal year summaries. Report: Harv-East.

———. Oregon state office, westside timber harvest report, fiscal year Summaries. Report: Harvest westside summary.

———. 1966. Public land statistics 1965. Washington, DC: US Department of the Interior.

———. 1988. Public land statistics 1987. Vol. 172. Washington, DC: US Department of the Interior.

———. 1989. Public land statistics 1988. Vol. 173. Washington, DC: US Department of the Interior.

———. 1990. Public land statistics 1989. Vol. 174. Washington, DC: US Department of the Interior.

————. 1991. Public land statistics 1990. Vol. 175. Washington, DC: US Department of the Interior.

————. 1992. Public land statistics 1991. Vol. 176. Washington, DC: US Department of the Interior.

————. 1993. Public land statistics 1992. Vol. 177. Washington, DC: US Department of the Interior.

————. 1994. Public land statistics 1993. Vol. 178. Washington, DC: US Department of the Interior.

————. 1996. Public land statistics 1994-95. Vols. 179-180. Washington, DC: US Department of the Interior.

————. 1997. Public land statistics 1996. Vol. 181. Washington, DC: US Department of the Interior.

————. 1985-87. Public land statistics 1984-86. Vols. 169-171. Washington, DC: US Department of the Interior.

————. 1983-84. Public land statistics 1982-83. Washington, DC: US Department of the Interior.

————. 1963-64. Public land statistics 1962-63. Washington, DC: US Department of the Interior.

FOREST SERVICE (FS). 1988. Report of the Forest Service, fiscal year 1987. Washington, DC: US Department of Agriculture.

————. 1989. Report of the Forest Service, fiscal year 1988. Washington, DC: US Department of Agriculture.

————. 1990. Report of the Forest Service, fiscal year 1989. Washington, DC: US Department of Agriculture.

————. 1991. Report of the Forest Service, fiscal year 1990. Washington, DC: US Department of Agriculture.

————. 1992. Report of the Forest Service, fiscal year 1991. Washington, DC: US Department of Agriculture.

————. 1993. Report of the Forest Service, fiscal year 1992. Washington, DC: US Department of Agriculture.

————. 1994. Report of the Forest Service, fiscal year 1993. Washington, DC: US Department of Agriculture.

————. 1995. Report of the Forest Service, fiscal year 1994. Washington, DC: US Department of Agriculture.

————. 1996. Report of the Forest Service, fiscal year 1995. Washington, DC: US Department of Agriculture.

————. 1997. Report of the Forest Service, fiscal year 1996. Washington, DC: US Department of Agriculture.

————. Report of the Forest Service, fiscal year[s] 1911-15, 1919-20, 1925, 1930, 1935, 1940, 1942, 1944-45, 1950-53, 1955, 1960, 1965, 1970. Washington, DC: US Department of Agriculture.

————. Report of the Forest Service, fiscal year[s] 1972-86. Washington, DC: US Department of Agriculture.

HAYES, N. 1996. Statement on implementation of the Northwest forest plan before the Subcommittee on National Parks, Forests, and Lands Committee on Resources, US House of Representatives. July 23.

Personal communication, 1997

BERG, K. Threatened and endangered species specialist, Bureau of Land Management. Washington, DC.

COSTELLO, T. Natural resource specialist, Bureau of Land Management. Denver, CO.

CULBERT, J. Budget assistant, USDA Forest Service. Washington, DC.

FIELDER, D. Forester, Bureau of Land Management. Washington, DC.

HOLTROP, J.D. Deputy director, USDA Forest Service. Washington, DC.

JANES, E. Senior water resources specialist, Bureau of Land Management. Washington DC.

LAFAYETTE, R. Riparian management and watershed improvement specialist, USDA Forest Service. Washington, DC.